THE RIGHT WAY TO SPELL

J. E. Metcalfe

CONTENTS

INTRODUCTION

According to examiners in English for the school examination boards, to tutors interviewing candidates for entrance to universities and polytechnics, and to employers trying to choose employees, one of the main deficiencies of those presenting themselves is in the understanding and appreciation of their own language. In the early nineteenth century, when comparatively few people were educated, shortcomings could be tolerated, but now the situation is entirely different. A leader-writer in a respected national newspaper has written: "There was once a dream that the culture of the fortunate should be everybody's culture. Today, when eyes are trained not on dull tasks but on duller entertainment, . . . that dream is exhausted."

Education is compulsory for all children, and young people are crowding into a growing number of universities and colleges. More books are published than ever before, and there are numerous libraries. The natural outcome, one might have innocently imagined, should have been an enlightened and literate society. Unfortunately expectations have not been realised, and we still find ourselves assailed by slipshod spoken and written English, careless spelling and mispronunciations. Even some teachers, we understand, are hazy in their knowledge and use of the language, and there are alarming reports that some education authorities favour a theory that neither grammar nor spelling matters, that "ability to communicate" is all-important. It is a pity that of the mass of published books many are worthless novels in which the standard of writing is atrocious, and the "media"—Press, television and radio—are no help, either, as models of English.

Nevertheless, the general depressing situation is lightened by repeated evidence that many people are genuinely interested in the encouragement of good standards in English. Some, perhaps aware of their own weaknesses, actually buy or borrow appropriate books, and I have been impressed by the popularity of my earlier book in this series, *The Right Way to Improve Your English*. Of that book, dealing mainly with grammatical aspects of the language, the present book is a continuation concentrating more on words and their spelling. There has been very little repetition, and that only where essential.

There are already several books dealing with spelling only, but as most of them consist largely of lists of words which can be found in dictionaries they are in a way superfluous. A book on spelling should be more; it should help the reader to enjoy the fascination of words *as words*, to induce an interest in their history, to appreciate how they are formed, to listen to their sounds, and to be aware of strange inconsistencies.

This book is offered not in a didactic manner but in a spirit of cooperation, assistance and gentle persuasion. While keeping the needs of the doubtful speller in the forefront of my mind I have given considerable attention to the formation of words. A general list of words at the end of the book—words which can raise doubts in spelling, words which can be misspelt, and words which are interesting—is preceded by notes on selected words which in my opinion deserve discursive comment.

Spelling is based on the alphabet, and I am glad to have this opportunity to quote from a delightful little book, *Origins of the Alphabet*, by Joseph Naveh (published by Cassell):

> "But bad as English spelling may be, it still retains most of the principles of alphabetic writing. It takes only a year or two of study to learn to spell English. The Chinese, on the other hand, have to devote many years to learning characters if they are to have a complete command of their literature."

You may be relieved, then, that you are not Chinese.

PART I

The Development of Spelling

It is, of course, *English* spelling (or *orthography*) with which we are concerned in this book. Users of other languages have their difficulties, too, so that English-writers unsure of their spelling need not think themselves unique. From books on French grammar published in France for French people, it is clear that many French find problems in their own language just as many English-speaking people find in English. I referred above to English-writers and not to English-speakers, for it is only in writing that incorrect spelling shows itself, and the most fluent speaker may be quite inadequate when he puts pen to paper.

The supremacy of English as a world language is a relic of the age when Great Britain was an important world power. The inhabitants of the huge chunks of territory which in old atlases were coloured red enjoyed the benefits of learning English from explorers, travellers, missionaries and settlers. It is rather remarkable that today, despite minor idiomatic and spelling differences, American custom, an infinity of verbal differences, and diverse political constitutions, there is general consistency in written English throughout the world.

It must be realised that speech is far, far older than writing. The development of written language in different parts of the world is an absorbing subject for which this is not the place, but, very briefly, it can be said that the symbols of language were formed to represent objects, actions or syllables of speech. The most convenient of these three representations was probably

11

found to be the third as it covered a wider field than the first
two, and in time representations developed into *characters* which
could be combined to form *words* and thus allowed greater
latitude than syllables. The first language to be written was
Sumerian, which began as simple pictures and which can be
traced as far back as 3100 B.C. (See, for example, *The Story of
Handwriting*, by Alfred Fairbank, published by Faber & Faber.)

The Canaanites are said to have developed the first *alphabet*
in the middle of the second millennium B.C. The convenience of
this method of writing led to its adoption by other Semitic
peoples and the ancient Greeks, and, while each nation developed
its own, the scripts were all based on Canaanite characters.
Today there are Hebrew, Greek, Cyrillic, Arabic and Latin
alphabets, besides the bewilderingly vast range of characters of
the Far East (China and Japan). The Latin or Roman alphabet,
now the most widely used in the world, is a derivative of archaic
Greek script. The word *alphabet* is so named from the first two
letters of the Greek alphabet, *alpha* and *beta*, which in turn
were named after the first two signs of the Phoenician alphabet
aleph and *beth*. Also derived from the Greek alphabet is Cyrillic
script, used in the Soviet Union, Bulgaria and Yugoslavia,
originally by members of the Orthodox Church, and called after
St. Cyril who died in A.D. 869.

With Julius Caesar's incursions into Britain in 55 and 54 B.C.,
the native Britons perhaps picked up a few Latin expressions
and words but, unlike the invaders, they knew nothing about
writing. What happened, then, to the only "real" British
languages which existed before the Romans came? These
languages, themselves derived from even older forms of speech,
were the original Celtic tongues, which, most remarkably, had
little effect on the development of English. Today they survive
in Gaelic, Irish, Welsh, Manx and Cornish, but not in English,
despite the fact that English is a mixture of several languages.

It was probably not until the beginning of the real Roman
occupation, about a hundred years after Julius Caesar, that the
Roman alphabet was introduced into Britain. For a few
centuries writing was practised by only monks and other
scholars, being chiefly for ecclesiastical and legal documents and
in Latin. We read so much today that it is difficult to imagine a

time when hardly anybody did any reading. For centuries people passed their time in other ways; perhaps they conversed far more than they do now, and stories would be told by travelling storytellers and bards. Even kings and other leaders had to employ scribes. Monks busied themselves in writing original works or copying others in beautiful manuscript, but "ordinary" people did not need to read them, even if they could.

The development of English took place over a very long time, during which most of the people in Britain were quite content with the spoken language, based on the speech of the sixth-century Anglo-Saxon invaders. Latin persisted, later invaders from Scandinavia brought much of their language, and the Norman Conquest of 1066 brought French. By the thirteenth century · three languages were in use—Latin for scholars, ecclesiastics, philosophers and lawyers, French for the aristocracy, and English for the rest.

The schools began teaching English about 1300 and English was at last permissible in the law courts in 1362. Gradually the various languages mingled, and Geoffrey Chaucer's *Canterbury Tales*, for example, probably written after 1373, were written in an attractive mixture of English and French. Chaucer has been accused of using too many French words as an affectation, but French was certainly more elegant, more melodious, than the written and spoken English of the time. Chaucer was not alone in trying to improve the language, and the following passage, written in 1385, not only shows the awareness of sensitive people to the imperfections of English but is an example of the extraordinary written language of the period:

"As it is knowe how meny maner peple beeth in this lond; there beeth also so many dyvers longages and tongs. Notheless Walsche men and Scots that beeth nought medled with other nations, holdeth wel nyh hir firste longage and speche; . . . but the Flemynges that woneth in the west side of Wales, having left her strange spech, and speketh sexonliche now. Also Englishe men, they had from the bygynnynge thre maner speche: northerns, sowtherne, and middel speche in the middel of the londe, as they come of three maner of peple of Germania: notheless by commyxtion and mellynge first with Danes, and afterwards with Normans, in meny the contrary longage is apayred [corrupted]. . . . All the longage of the Northumbers, and specialliche at York, is so scharp, flitting and frotynge, and unschape, that we southerne men may that langage unethe understonde."

"Modern" English is generally accepted as having originated about 1500, since when it has been enriched by countless influences and additions from many other languages.

The innovation which did more than anything to encourage the use of writing, and *eventually* to encourage more people to learn to read, was the invention of printing in the middle of the fifteenth century. Latin was still the language of the learned, and most of the early printed books were in Latin. Then, with the influx of other languages, came the development of written English with its confused vagaries of spelling. Before the introduction of printing one or two monks in their manuscripts had attempted spelling reforms, but when the printers came on the scene they had authors at their mercy. Between 1480 and 1660 they had become accustomed to their own conventions, and ideas of "correct" and "incorrect" spelling were not considered. William Caxton and other early printers tended to adopt the Middle English word patterns of the scribes without, however, any standardisation.

The gradual spread of literacy from the sixteenth century, accompanied by a surge in the publication of printed matter, led a number of scholars to appreciate that inconsistency was an embarrassment. Inconsistency, of course, is still with us, and it can baffle many people. Why, for example, should *English* itself sound as if it began with an *I*? The word *England* is derived from *Engla-land*, the land of the Angles or Engles, not the Ingles. Numerous other examples of inconsistency in pronunciation and spelling could be cited, but examples which spring readily to mind are the following: *clerk, jerk*; *full, dull*; *work, fork*; *worm, form*; *put, but*; *gone, done, bone*; *four, dour*; *said, laid, plaid*; *cow, low*; *treat, threat*; the two meanings of *tear*; the two tenses of *read*; *names, Thames*; *love, strove*; and all the different sounds made by *-ough*.

Inconsistencies such as these, which contribute to the fascination of the language, infuriate only those people who have no real love for it and would seek to impoverish it by revolutionary spelling reform. If there must be reform, let it evolve gradually. In the late nineteenth century and the early twentieth century there were some successful official attempts at spelling modification in France, Italy and Germany, but these were in the nature of standardisation rather than spelling reform.

After the monks' vain pursuit of orthographical perfection in Britain (to which I have referred) the first potential reformer was Sir Thomas Smith, who in 1568 published a book (in Latin!) on English spelling. He was followed by several other scholars in the sixteenth and seventeenth centuries, but there is no space here for details of their activities. Interested readers can find fascinating accounts of the development of the language in two excellent books—*Something About Words* by Ernest Weekley (John Murray) and *Our Language* by Simeon Potter (Penguin Books). I also recommend the many volumes of "The Language Library" published by André Deutsch and the light-hearted word books of Ivor Brown published by Jonathan Cape.

Interest in spelling reform was revived in the 1840s, largely through the work of Sir Isaac Pitman. His scheme for reform was rivalled by others but none found acceptance, perhaps because there were too many. There have been attempts at reform in this century, not only by the Simplified Spelling Society but also by Robert Bridges (Poet Laureate from 1912 to 1930) and George Bernard Shaw. In 1961 Sir James Pitman (Isaac's grandson) introduced his Initial Teaching Alphabet, which, however, is not a reformed spelling system but a teaching method.

Several dictionaries appeared before the publication of Dr. Samuel Johnson's in 1755, and although this great work contained many inconsistencies it established the basis of our spelling of today, which we accept with all its imperfections. If doubtful spellers sometimes feel that they are lost in a jungle they need not be ashamed of their inadequate sense of direction. Rules of orientation in a jungle being less arbitrary than so-called rules of spelling, I have a mild resentment against the word "rules" and prefer to think of "accepted practices".

The term "rules", however, is shorter and more convenient to use, and at this stage in our study you may ask: "Who made the rules?" Even as late as the eighteenth century many people did not seem to concern themselves greatly with rules or accepted practices, the general feeling perhaps being that as long as a writer's meaning was understood, spelling did not matter. Ephraim Chambers in his *Cyclopaedia* (1743) wrote:

"In the English, the orthography is more vague and unascertained, than in any other language we know of. Every author, and almost every printer, has his particular system. Nay, it is scarce so well with us as that: we not only differ from one another; but there is scarce any that consists with himself. The same word shall frequently appear with two or three different faces in the same page, not to say line."

As the English-speaking world became more organised, as communications developed, as more people became educated, as trade intensified, as ability to read and write became essential, as competition grew, as people's outlooks broadened, as travel became practicable, it became evident that discipline and consistency in spelling became not only desirable but necessary. Writers realised that there must be no doubt about meaning, and elimination of doubt could be made possible by observing a certain consistency in spelling.

Observance of consistency led to the limited formulation of rules. Most of the rules developed from within, out of tradition, convention, general understanding and common practice. The rules were not imposed from without, and it is noteworthy that there is no organisation in Great Britain similar to the two language academies of Italy (founded in 1582) and France (founded in 1635). There are various bodies which concern themselves with language, such as the British Academy, the Philological Society and the English Association, but, admirable though these institutions are, they do not give *authoritative* linguistic advice in the manner of the two Continental Academies. The members of the French Academy, for example, meet periodically to *decide*—amongst many other matters concerned with the French language—how words, especially new words, are to be spelt.

Agreement to stick to rules developed in the nineteenth century, when more people discovered the joys of reading and writing. Hand-in-hand with the Industrial Revolution came a surge in the publication of books, newspapers, periodicals and the transactions of learned societies. The necessity of discipline in spelling was accompanied by an appreciation of discipline in grammar, but grammar is different from spelling as much of it depends on logical thought, and most of the great writers of the past, however loose their spelling (and unlike many of today's ephemeral writers) were good grammarians.

In spite of the evolution of rules in spelling there are anomalies which cannot be satisfactorily explained, such as alternative spellings for some words and a deliberate legality in the breaking of some rules. Some irregularities are legacies of the past, perhaps results of writers' or printers' carelessness which, unnoticed at the time, have been assimilated into the written language.

American spelling is a subject with which I shall deal later, but it is necessary to say something about American English in general. Some people accustomed to British English appear to resent, even occasionally be enraged by, American spelling, pronunciation, usage, phraseology, idiom and meanings. Such emotion is unjustified, for the Americans have had over three hundred years to develop their own kind of English. When we consider the history of America—at least the history since the arrival of the Europeans—and the mixture of the races that have made it, we should be flattered that they have adopted *our* language and no other nation's.

The English introduced into Virginia in 1607 and into Massachusetts in 1620 was the English of the seventeenth century, and naturally the subsequent evolution followed by the language in America differed somewhat from the evolution followed in Britain. I find it surprising that after three and a half centuries the two kinds of English have so much in common, for it is only in this century that the speed of communication has tended to neutralise the differences between the two. With global increase of American influence, some parts of the world have adopted American English simply because they have known no other. American English (in which I include spelling) cannot be dismissed as "wrong", and we cannot criticise our American friends for using it.

As far as American spelling is concerned, it must not be thought that it has been allowed to develop haphazardly. The

American spelling of today, on the whole, is the result of years of deliberation, of trial and error, of advance and retreat, the result of labour initiated by the great lexicographer Noah Webster (1758–1843). Webster made several attempts at standardisation, would discard, revive and discard again until he, and his successors, reached forms of spelling that were to be adopted as standard American, forms which in many cases are more logical than our own.

To conclude this chapter it may be entertaining to quote from a work by John Hart, a disciple of the reformer Sir Thomas Smith to whom I have referred. Published in 1569, the work bore the long title *An Orthographie conteyning the due order and reason, howe to paint thimage of mannes voice, most like to the life or nature*. Hart wrote:

"But in the moderne and present maner of writing (aswell of certaine other languages as of our English) there is such confusion and disorder, as it may be accounted rather a kinde of ciphring, or such a darke kinde of writing, as the best and readiest wit that ever hath bene, could, or that is or shalbe, can or may, by the only gift of reason, attaine to the ready and perfite reading thereof, without a long and tedious labour, for that it is unfit and wrong shapen for the proportion of the voice."

PART II

Word-Formation

Anybody really interested in spelling will naturally want to know how words are formed and how, despite numerous inconsistencies, the mode of formation can influence the spelling. Some people have an innate instinct for words, but others not so blessed can develop a retentive visual memory and keep it in sound working condition by intelligent reading. A "good speller" need not be well versed in etymology, but the detection of irregularities and similarities, and awareness of their existence, add to the fun of language-study. Notes on the formation of words, therefore, will be necessary as a foundation, and remarks on the "rules" will be given where appropriate.

WORD-CONVERSIONS

Basic words are generally changed into related words by the addition of prefixes or suffixes, more often by suffixes. In the case of verbs, for example, *talk* (present tense) becomes *talked* (past tense and past participle) and *talking* (present participle). I say "generally" because "rules" of grammar and of spelling are often disturbed by exceptions. *Eat*, for instance, gives *ate*, not "eated", *sit* gives *sat*, *hold* gives *held*, and *sleep* gives *slept*.

In this book I shall use the expression "basic verb" rather than "indicative" and terms like "infinitive" and "present tense, first person". Technical terms will be avoided as far as possible, but it will be essential to use "past tense", "past participle" and "present participle". The meaning of past tense, generally understood, is obvious, but some of my readers may have forgotten about participles. In "I am waiting", *waiting* is the present participle of the verb *to wait*, and in "I have waited" *waited* is the past participle.

It will be evident from the examples to be given later that past participles can take many forms, but for a great many verbs the past participle is the same as the past tense, examples being: "I passed", "I have passed", "You worked", "You have worked". The verb *pass* leads to the versatile derivative *past*, which can serve as noun, adjective, preposition, adverb and past participle. Although the usual past participle of *pass* is *passed*, with the verb *to have* ("He has passed the post"), *past* can be used as a past participle with the verb *to be* ("The hard times are past").

Other past participles ending in *t* are *leapt* (from *leap*), *burnt* (from *burn*) and *dreamt* (from *dream*). It is true that in practice these past participles are often interchanged with the past tenses—*leaped, burned* and *dreamed*—but to distinguish one from the other it is preferable to end the past participles with *t*.

Despite the vagaries of the past participle, the present participle is constant, always ending in *ing* and presenting no spelling puzzles.

I apologise for this diversion which to many readers will be elementary, but, as Sir Thomas Beecham observed (in effect), no matter how often Beethoven's Fifth Symphony is played there is always someone who is hearing it for the first time. Moreover, as this is a book mainly on spelling and words rather than on grammar, I need not deal here with future tense and conditional and subjunctive moods which in English do not form special words as they do (for example) in French.

Basic verbs ending in consonants

For weak spellers, the rules for converting the present tense of verbs into past tense, past participle and present participle can appear so involved that it is easier to remember the "look" of the words themselves than to try to remember the rules. The addition of *ed* or *ing* to the present tense sometimes needs a connecting link, and the nature of the link (according to the rules) depends on the structure of the basic word and the placing of the stressed syllable.

Verbs of one short (unsustained) syllable ending in a consonant are usually converted by doubling the last letter before the *ed* or *ing*. Thus we get: *hug, hugged, hugging*; *pet, petted, petting*; *trap, trapped, trapping*. One exception is *tread*, which gives *trod* (past tense), *trodden* (past participle) and *treading* (present participle). Other strange exceptions are *cut* and *put*, where the past tense and past participle are still *cut* and *put* but the present participles *cutting* and *putting*. *Jut*, on the other hand (just to be awkward), gives *jutted* and *jutting*. Yet another inconsistent *u* verb is *run*, with its past tense *ran*, its past participle *run*, and its present participle *running*.

Where the monosyllable is sustained (or long) the final consonant remains single, but there are inconsistencies. *Lead* and *read* might be expected to behave similarly, yet the past tenses and past participles are *led* and *read*. *Feed* and *need* make *fed* and *needed*. *Bear* and *near* (in the sense of "nearing one's goal") should follow parallel paths, but *bear* makes *bore* (past tense), *borne* (past participle) and *bearing* (present participle), while *near* follows the regular pattern of *neared* (past tense and past participle) and *nearing* (present participle). (The spelling of the past participle, *borne*, distinguishes it from *born* in the sense of birth.)

The monosyllabic verb *bid* is used in two senses, the normal sense and the auction sense. In the normal sense, the past tense is *bade* and the past participle *bidden* ("I bade him come" and "I have bidden him to come"). In the auction sense, the past tense and past participle are both *bid* ("I bid ten pounds for it" and "I have bid for it").

Still on the subject of exceptions, I must draw attention to the verb *lend*, of which the related noun is *loan*. Corrupt usage has developed the practice of adopting *loan* as a verb, so that one frequently hears sentences like these: "He loaned me a fiver", "He is loaning me a fiver". It is all right to make a *loan* (noun), but the correct forms of the verb *lend* are *lent* (past tense and past participle) and *lending* (present participle).

The past tense and past participle of *bend* are both *bent*, but occasionally you may hear the archaic (old-fashioned) form *bended*, as in "on my bended knees".

Verbs of two syllables (occasionally three) ending in a hard consonant take the final double consonant if the stress is on the second (or last) syllable, as in: *abut, abutted, abutting*; *overlap, overlapped, overlapping*; *prod, prodded, prodding*; *regret, regretted, regretting*. If the stress is on the first syllable of a basic two-syllable verb the final consonant usually stays single, as in: *gallop, galloped, galloping*; *limit, limited, limiting*. The rule breaks down in the case of (for example) *ballot*, where, although the stress is on the first syllable, the related words *ballotted* and *ballotting* have a double *t*. Likewise there are *combat, combatted* and *combatting*, and *rivet, rivetted* and *rivetting*.

In the three-syllable verbs *elicit* and *solicit*, where the stress is on the middle syllable, the *t* stays single to give *elicited, eliciting, solicited* and *soliciting*. Shorter *-it* verbs are inconsistent. Although *sit* makes *sat* and *sitting*, the past tense and past participle of *quit* are both *quitted*, and the present participle *quitting* agrees with *sitting*. ("I have quit" is said colloquially.) As for *hit*, "hitted" would sound strange, and the past tense and past participle are both *hit*, with *hitting* as the present participle. The verbs *emit, fit, grit* and *knit* all follow the *-itted* and *-itting* pattern.

There are several nouns and adjectives ending in *ight* but few verbs. Examples of verbs which spring to mind are: *alight* (in the sense of getting off a vehicle); *delight*; *light*; *right* (righting a wrong); and *sight*. All follow the *-ighted* and *-ighting* pattern, but in the case of the verb *light* the past tense and past participle can be *lighted* or *lit*.

Basic verbs ending in y

With most basic verbs ending in *y* after a consonant or after *h* (not that there are many) the past tense and past participle are obtained by substituting the *y* by *ied*, but in the present participle the *y* is retained and *ing* is added. Examples are: *chivvy, chivvied, chivvying*; *cry, cried, crying*; *lobby, lobbied, lobbying*; *ply, plied, plying*; *shy, shied, shying*.

If the *y* follows a vowel it is not normally dropped, and we have: *betray, betrayed, betraying*; *cloy, cloyed, cloying*; *play, played, playing*; *toy, toyed, toying*. There are exceptions; for example, *buy* gives *bought* and *buying*, and *-ay* exceptions are *say* (*said*), *pay* (*paid*) and *lay* (*laid*).

Other examples of doubling

I have given a few examples of the doubling of the final consonants *d*, *g*, *p* and *t*. Other consonants which are usually (but not always) doubled after appearing as single last letters are *b*, *l*, *m*, *n*, *r* and *s*, but there is option in two *s* cases as the following examples will show:

Case	Basic verb	Past tense and past participle	Present participle
b	ebb	ebbed	ebbing
b	rob	robbed	robbing
b	stab	stabbed	stabbing
m	dim	dimmed	dimming
m	gum	gummed	gumming
m	ram	rammed	ramming
n	ban	banned	banning
n	shun	shunned	shunning
n	sin	sinned	sinning
r	abhor	abhorred	abhorring
r	demur	demurred	demurring
r	occur	occurred	occurring
s	gas	gassed	gassing
s	bias	biased *or* biassed	biasing *or* biassing
s	focus	focused *or* focussed	focusing *or* focussing

Exceptions include verbs ending in *en* (such as *open*, *opened* and *opening*, and *sharpen*, *sharpened* and *sharpening*), and verbs ending in *er* (such as *offer*, *offered* and *offering*, and *temper*, *tempered* and *tempering*). The irregular verb *run* (*ran*, *running*) was mentioned earlier, and another irregular verb is *win* (*won*, *winning*).

Inadequate spellers often find difficulty in deciding whether to put one *r* or two in *occurred*, *occurring*, *recurred* and *recurring*. There is never any doubt about the spelling of *gassed* and *gassing*, but *biased*, *biasing*, *focused* and *focusing* are more commonly spelt with one *s*.

Basic verbs ending in l

The following are examples of British practice (not necessarily American):

Basic verb	Past tense and past participle	Present participle	Related noun (if any)
l preceded by one vowel:			
cancel	cancelled	cancelling	cancellation
gel	gelled	gelling	
travel	travelled	travelling	travel
l preceded by two vowels:			
feel	felt	feeling	feeling
heal	healed	healing	
kneel	knelt	kneeling	
maul	mauled	mauling	
sail	sailed	sailing	
steal	stole (*past participle* stolen)	stealing	
l preceded by a vowel and a consonant:			
crawl	crawled	crawling	crawl
curl	curled	curling	curl
harl	harled	harling	
trawl	trawled	trawling	trawl
l doubled already:			
cull	culled	culling	cull
pall	palled	palling	
sell	sold	selling	sale
spell	spelled (*past participle* spelt)	spelling	
tell	told	telling	

Some verbs can be spelt with one *l* or two, but the past tense and the participles have the double *l*, examples being *enthral(l)* and *marshal(l)*. Further examples of the construction of words based on verbs ending in *l* or *ll* are given on page 87.

A favourite example of irregularity with verbs ending in *l* is *parallel*, of which the past tense has a single *l* to give *paralleled*. (Although *parallel* is usually an adjective, it is also used as a verb.) This irregularity conforms with standard American practice, which allows the final *l* in all such verbs to remain single. It is curious, in passing, to note that the epithet *unparalleled* is used far more often than *paralleled*, as in "unparalleled magnificence".

Basic verbs ending in e

Basic verbs ending in *e* usually take *d* for the past tense, as in *elope(d)*, *love(d)*, *moralise(d)*, *rule(d)*. For the present participle the *e* is dropped and replaced by *ing* (*eloping, loving, moralising, ruling*), but special cases are dealt with below.

Exceptions include *take*, of which the past tense is *took* but the past participle *taken* and the present participle *taking*. By this system, *make* should be converted to "mook" and "maken", but by one of our pleasant little quirks the past tense and past participle are *made*, in spite of consistency in *making*. Another exception is *hide*, of which the past tense is *hid*, the past participle *hidden*, and the present participle *hiding*. *Chide* should behave similarly but has alternatives, its past tense being *chided* or *chid*, its past participle *chided* or *chidden*, and its present participle *chiding*.

Another exception is *bite*, of which the past tense is *bit* (not "bited"), the past participle *bitten*, and the present participle *biting*. For *prove* the past tense is always *proved*, but there is another past participle, *proven*, which has a limited use in technical and legal language.

From *strike* are derived *struck* (past tense and usual past participle) and *striking* (present participle). An archaic form of past participle, *stricken*, is sometimes found in such sentences as "I am stricken in years" and such hackneyed expressions as "poverty-stricken" and "panic-stricken". These applications exemplify the common use of old-fashioned words by people who do not think about them. Another good example is provided by the obsolescent *bereft* (from *bereave*), as in "I was bereft of my senses". Even the commonest verbs can display irregularities. Thus, the past tense of *come* is *came* but the past participle is still *come*. The past tense and past participle of *lose* are both *lost*.

Verbs ending in eave

I referred above to the derivation of *bereft* from *bereave*, which means "to deprive, rob, spoil, or render desolate". In its association with the death of near relatives the past participle has gradually been replaced in popular usage by *bereaved*, which means the same. In *The Tempest* Ariel speaks to the King of Naples about Ferdinand: "Thee of thy son, Alonso,/They have bereft; . . ."

Disagreement among the *-eave* words is shown in the following list, and in some cases an alternative form of the past tense or past participle is permissible. The present participle follows the regular *-ing* construction with the e dropped. *Cleave*, incidentally, has two meanings which in a sense are opposites: (1) to split asunder; (2) to adhere.

Basic verb	Past tense	Past participle	Present participle
bereave	bereaved	bereaved *or* bereft	bereaving
cleave (1)	cleaved, clove *or* cleft	cloven *or* cleft	cleaving
cleave (2)	cleaved *or* clave	cleaved	cleaving
heaved	heaved *or* hove	heaved *or* hove	heaving
leave	left	left	leaving
reave	reaved *or* reft	reaved *or* reft	reaving
weave	wove	woven	weaving

Common expressions using the archaic forms of the *cleave* (1) words are "cloven hoof" and "in a cleft stick", where the past participle serves as an adjective. *Heave* has a nautical sense in "Heave to" and "The boat hove in sight". Although the past participle of *weave* is *woven* commerce talks about "wove paper", "finely-wove fabric" and many other woven materials.

Special cases of -ing

The doubtful speller often finds difficulty in deciding whether or not to retain the final e in converting the present tense of a verb to the present participle. For example, in that sentence, why did I not write "decideing" when *decide* ends in *e*?

Some words are easy, and nobody gives a thought to common words like *dying* and *tying* from *die* and *tie*. *Dyeing* and *singeing*, likewise, should present no problems; if the *e* were omitted the results would be *dying* and *singing*, which are words already. Another irregularity is seen in the verb *hie* ("Hie you thither"), of which the past tense is certainly *hied*. *Hying* is given as the present participle in some dictionaries, but the usual spelling is *hieing*.

The *e* is retained in some cases, as in *swingeing* ("swingeing increases in inflation") and *shoeing*. Curiously, *ageing* is right but so are *foraging, managing* and *raging*.

Centre, when used as a verb, gives *centred* as past tense and past participle, but some people are puzzled about the present participle. Should it be *centreing* or (as the Americans have it) *centering*? The accepted spelling in British English is *centring*, with the *e* dropped. Verbs of similar construction include *accoutre* (*accoutring*), *manoeuvre* (*manoeuvring*) and *mitre* (*mitring*).

Verbs ending in *c* are given a gratuitous *k*, as in *bivouac(king)*, *panic(king), picnic(king)* and *mimic(king)*.

The needs of modern English have given rise to certain verbs from nouns which were originally considered only as nouns. *Service*, for instance, led to the *servicing* of cars and many other things, and the invention of the *torpedo* made *torpedoing* necessary. These spellings have developed from common custom, the accepted past tense and past participle being *serviced* and *torpedoed*. To put something through a *process* is now a verb *to process*, with *processed* as past tense and past participle and *processing* as present participle.

In most cases there is nothing reprehensible in the adoption of nouns as verbs with the same spelling, for the practice can be convenient and save circumlocution. If on the other hand the use of a noun as a verb grates on the ear it should be avoided. "I am taking a bus home" is more pleasant than "I am bussing home", but "bussing" seems to be used in the United States. I have already referred to the malpractice of using *loan* as a verb instead of *lend*.

Though it has nothing to do with spelling, I want to mention a deplorable speech habit (which seems to be confined to the English Midlands and the south) associated with -*ing* words like *drawing*. The habit is to insert an intrusive *r* to produce the horrible "drawring"; the guilty people, who seem to be unaware of it, are often the same people who must always separate two consecutive vowels by a non-existent *r*.

Verbs ending in vowel sounds

Reference to the noun and verb *torpedo* naturally leads to the consideration of other verbs ending in the vowel sound *o*. Apart from *torpedo*, only three need to be considered, of which two are from nouns, *radio* and *veto*. *Radio* is given an *e* in *radioed* but not in the present participle *radioing*. *Veto* is similar, giving *vetoed* and *vetoing*.

The third is one of the most frequently used verbs in the language, *go*. Dealing with *come*, I remarked that even the commonest verbs can show irregularities, and *go* is as irregular as *come*. Its past tense is *went* (not a bit like *go*), its past participle *gone*, and its present participle *going*.

Some other verbs are less common. *Shanghai* (to get a man drunk and put him aboard a ship needing a crew), for instance, nowadays has little need of application. If its past tense and participles must be used, the forms are *shanghaied* and *shanghaieing*. Some people prefer the apostrophe to *e*, as in *shanghai'd* and *shanghai'ing*. Even less commonly heard or read is the past participle (used as an adjective) *moustachioed* or *moustachio'd*.

Basic verbs ending in ive

Basic verbs ending in *ive* are regular or irregular. By "regular" I mean verbs of which the past tense and past participle are made by adding *d* to the basic verb and the present participle by dropping the *e* and adding *ing*. Examples of regular -*ive* verbs are: *connive, connived, conniving*; *dive, dived, diving*; *live, lived, living*. Examples of irregular -*ive* verbs are given in the following list:

Basic verb	Past tense	Past participle	Present participle
drive	drove	driven	driving
give	gave	given	giving

Basic verb	Past tense	Past participle	Present participle
rive	rived	riven	riving
shrive	shrove	shriven	shriving
strive	strove	striven	striving
thrive	thrived or throve	thrived or thriven	thriving

There are, of course, many other English verbs ending in *ive*, and the above are given only as examples of regularity and irregularity. The unique pronunciation of *give* and *live* (different from that of other *-ive* verbs) is one of the charming oddities of the language. The Scots have a special verb, *to gift*, meaning to give or bequeath a handsome contribution to a worthy cause.

Basic verbs ending in w

Basic verbs ending in *w*, too, are regular or irregular in pattern. By "regular" in this case I mean the pattern in which the past tense and past participle are made by adding *ed* to the basic verb and the present participle by adding *ing*. Examples of regular *-w* verbs are: *brew, brewed, brewing*; *endow, endowed, endowing*; *row, rowed, rowing*; *view, viewed, viewing*. Examples of irregular *-w* verbs are listed below:

Basic verb	Past tense	Past participle	Present participle
draw	drew	drawn	drawing
grow	grew	grown	growing
hew	hewed	hewn	hewing
sew	sewed	sewn	sewing
show	showed	shown	showing
strew	strewed	strewn	strewing
throw	threw	thrown	throwing

I should point out that, although *crow* now follows the regular pattern of *crowed* and *crowing*, the archaic past tense *crew* is not to be ignored. ("And immediately the cock crew." Matthew, xxvi. 74, *A.V.*)

Shew as an alternative to *show* is obsolete, even if still seen occasionally.

Basic verbs containing i with n

Some people are confused when they have to use the past tense or past participle of certain verbs containing the vowel *i* followed by *n*. They struggle mentally as they wonder if they should write or say "I sank it" or "I sunk it", when they know that "I wrang my washing" sounds all wrong. Their confusion is excusable, for such verbs are infuriatingly inconsistent.

The only *-in* verb which follows a normal pattern is *sin*, from which even the similar *win* differs. *Wring*, with past tense *wrung*, is different even from *ring*, with past tense *rang*.

Apart from *-in* verbs there is *swim*, which I have included in the list below as it is similar in behaviour to some of the *-in* verbs.

Basic verb	Past tense	Past participle	Present participle
begin	began	begun	beginning
bring	brought	brought	bringing
cling	clung	clung	clinging
drink	drank	drunk	drinking
fling	flung	flung	flinging
ring	rang	rung	ringing
shrink	shrank	shrunk	shrinking
sin	sinned	sinned	sinning
sing	sang	sung	singing
sink	sank	sunk	sinking
spin	spun	spun	spinning
spring	sprang	sprung	springing
swim	swam	swum	swimming
swing	swung	swung	swinging
think	thought	thought	thinking
win	won	won	winning
wring	wrung	wrung	wringing

The past participles *drunk, shrunk* and *sunk* have alternative forms used as adjectives: *drunken* ("drunken man"), *shrunken* ("shrunken head") and *sunken* ("sunken garden").

You must not be misled by Byron, who wrote:
"The isles of Greece, the isles of Greece!
Where burning Sappho loved and sung,
Where grew the arts of war and peace,
Where Delos rose, and Phoebus sprung!"

The past tense of *spin* has an archaic form, *span*, as in John

Ball's rhetoric of 1381, "When Adam delved and Eve span ..."

CONVERSION OF VERBS TO NOUNS

Some verbs can be changed into nouns simply by a change of spelling. From the verb *pursue*, for example, the noun is *pursuit*, and *sue* leads to *suit*. The noun from the verb *breathe* is *breath*, and the noun from *die* is *death*. *Inquire* (or *enquire*) leads to *inquiry* (or *enquiry*).

Many other verbs can be converted to nouns only by the addition of suffixes, in some cases with slight modifications. While to some extent one carries out a conversion unconsciously it is interesting and entertaining to review the various suffixes which have appeared in our language: *-ment, -ion, -tion; -ant, -ent; -ance, -ence; -ism, -ysis, -asm; -al; -age; -ry, -ery; -ure; -acy; -er, -ster; -ar; -ing; -ee, -and.*

-ment, -ion, -tion

Some verbs can take either of the two suffixes *-ment* and *-ion*, but the meanings of the two resulting formations are usually different. For example, *commitment* and *commission*, both from *commit*, have different meanings; *excitement* and *excitation*, both from *excite*, are different; and *complement* and *completion*, both from *complete*, are different.

The *-ment* ending is usually straightforward, being simply attached to the basic verb. With verbs ending in consonants, for example, there are: *amend(ment); detach(ment); embellish(ment); harass(ment); resent(ment).* With verbs ending in *e* there are: *abate(ment); defile(ment); encase(ment); incite(ment).* An exception is *argue*, the final *e* of which is dropped to give *argument.*

There is no need for *bewilder(ment)* if you come across *retiral*, which is the Scottish equivalent of *retirement.*

The *-ment* suffix cannot be discussed without a reference to those verbs ending in *dge*, such as *abridge, acknowledge, judge* and *lodge*. Although the conversions of all these are often spelt with the *e* included (*abridgement, acknowledgement, judgement, lodgement*), a common practice is to omit it from the first three (*abridgment, acknowledgment, judgment*) and include it only in *lodgement*. The Americans nearly always omit the *e*.

Normally, the *-ion* suffix is simply added to the basic verb, as in *collect(ion)*, *obstruct(ion)*, *repress(ion)*. Where the basic verb ends in *e*, the *e* is dropped, as in: *accumulate, accumulation*; *devote, devotion*; *pollute, pollution*; *secrete, secretion*.

There are numerous special cases. The noun from the verb *destroy* is *destruction*, and many thriller-writers have licensed themselves to use an unpleasant back-formation verb "destruct". ("Read the message quickly, for it will self-destruct in one minute".) *Recognize* should make "recognizion", but the noun is *recognition*. *Reconcile* makes the long noun *reconciliation*, and *resolve* makes *resolution*.

While on the subject of the *-ion* suffix for conversion of verbs to nouns I must deal with the verbs ending in *-tend*: *contend, distend, extend, intend, portend* and *pretend*. Uncertain spellers (understandably) often find difficulty with these, as the derived nouns follow no consistent pattern. There may be a problem in choosing between *s* and *t*, and the following list shows the correct conversions:

Basic verb	*Derived noun*
contend	contention
distend	distension
extend	extension
intend	intention
portend	portent
pretend	pretension

Extend is also related to the noun *extent*, which has a different meaning from *extension*. *Pretend* is related to *pretence*, which is not quite the same as *pretension* and not the same as the continuing state of *pretentiousness* (a noun derived from the adjective *pretentious*).

As adjectives have entered our discussion it is appropriate to point out that the adjective from *contend* is *contentious*, and this leads to another noun *contentiousness*. Although the verb *portend* gives the noun *portent* the adjective is *portentous* (often mispronounced "portentious"), and this gives another noun *portentousness*.

We have seen that the noun *destruction* comes from the verb *destroy.* *Construction*, however, is from *construct*, and *instruction* from *instruct*.

The noun *declension*, strangely, is derived not from an imaginary "declend" but from *decline*, a word which has several different meanings as a verb and is also used as a noun. *Prevention* is derived from *prevent*; there is no problem about this, but the preferred adjective is *preventive*, not, as many seem to think, the longer "preventative".

It is a mystery to many that while the noun from *adopt* is *adoption* the noun from *adapt* is *adaptation*, although the incorrect "adaption" is sometimes seen and heard. The verb *absorb* is unique in the replacement of its *b* by *p* to form *absorption.*

A note on the conflict between *-ection* and *-exion* will be found on page 88.

Numerous verbs in English end in *ate*, and for conversion to nouns the *e* is dropped and replaced by *ion*. A few examples are given here for the sake of illustration (from *illustrate*): *demonstrate, demonstration*; *enumerate, enumeration*; *meditate, meditation*; *pollinate, pollination*; *stagnate, stagnation.*

The suffix *-ation* is applied to some verbs ending in *ise*; for example: *authorise, authorisation*; *civilise, civilisation*; *improvise, improvisation*; *polarise, polarisation*. Conversion to the noun in each case requires the dropping of the final *e.* (The question of *-ise* and *-ize* is discussed on page 85.)

The suffix *-ation* can be a suffix in its own right even when the verb does *not* end in *ate*, examples (apart from *adaptation* mentioned above) being: *afforest, afforestation*; *crown, coronation*; *deprive, deprivation*; *derive, derivation*; *divine, divination*; *fix, fixation*; *inhale, inhalation.* It is obvious that where the verb ends in *e* the *e* is dropped in the conversion.

(It is curious, incidentally, that, although *derive* makes *derivation*, *contrive* makes *contrivance* and *survive* makes *survival*—three different suffixes used with similar verbs).

Still on the subject of the suffix *-ation*, it is interesting to observe that in the case of verbs ending in *ke* the *ke* is replaced by *c* before the suffix in the conversion to give the following nouns: *convoke, convocation*; *evoke, evocation*; *invoke, invocation*;

provoke, provocation; *revoke, revocation*. *Revoke* also makes the nouns *revocability* and *irrevocability*.

Where some basic verbs end in *ain* or *aim* the *i* is dropped to give, for example: *declaim, declamation*; *exclaim, exclamation*; *explain, explanation*; *proclaim, proclamation*. Other verbs in this group behave differently, such as: *abstain, abstention*; *entertain, entertainment*; *maintain, maintenance*; *sustain, sustenance*.

It might have been thought that the verb *remonstrate* would have led without question to the noun "remonstration", just as *demonstrate* gives *demonstration*. So it does, but this word is hardly ever used. The common noun is *remonstrance*, a word with a history which is given on page 132.

There is a wide range of *-ation* nouns derived from verbs, but here I want to deal with four in particular—those from the verbs *announce, denounce, enounce* and *pronounce*. *Announce* makes two nouns, *announcement* and *annunciation*, but the second is used almost solely in reference to the announcement of the Incarnation made by the Archangel Gabriel to the Virgin Mary. It will be noticed that in the conversion to this noun the *o* has been dropped before the *u*, and the same practice is followed in conversion to the nouns *denunciation, enunciation* and *pronunciation*. The last is a fairly common word, yet (and in spite of its meaning) some people persist in mispronouncing it "pronounciation". There is also a noun *pronouncement*, usually taken to mean an important announcement, a proclamation.

In the case of some nouns ending in *ation* there is another possible ending, *ative*, which does not give the same meaning as the *ation* ending. Examples are: *accuse, accusation, accusative*; *affirm, affirmation, affirmative*; *derive, derivation, derivative*; *indicate, indication, indicative*; *preserve, preservation, preservative*. *Direct* gives not "directation" but *direction* and *directive*.

There is another series of *-ation* nouns, admittedly rather long nouns because of their construction, which are derived from verbs ending in *ify* which in turn are derived from other, shorter, nouns. In each case the *y* is dropped and replaced by *ication*. A few examples among many such constructions are: *beatify, beatification*; *gasify, gasification*; *glory, glorification*; *sanctify, sanctification*; *solidify, solidification*.

Not surprisingly, there are exceptions. The noun *liquid* leads to the verb *liquefy*, not "liquify", and the verb leads in turn to *liquefaction*, not "liquidification". (For further notes on derivatives from *liquid*, the reader is referred to page 74.) The verb *putrefy* (not "putrify") leads to the noun *putrefaction*. The verb *crucify* leads to neither "crucification" nor "crucifaction" but to *crucifixion*. Although *perform* gives *performance*, *deform* gives *deformation*. Although *condole* gives *condolence*, *console* gives *consolation*.

Besides *-ation* nouns there are nouns in which the *tion* is preceded by other vowels, and I have already dealt with the dropping of the final *e* from basic verbs in their conversion to such nouns. The following notes are an extension of the discussion, with, when appropriate, remarks on special cases.

The verb *complete* forms, besides *completion*, two other nouns with different meanings—*completeness* and *complement*. *Complement* is often confused with *compliment*, and I shall have more to say about it later (page 115).

The suffix *-ition* is attached to several verbs ending in *ish*, where *sh* is dropped and replaced by *ition*. Thus, *abolish* is converted to *abolition*, *admonish* to *admonition*, and *demolish* to *demolition*. The suffix is not limited to *-ish* verbs, however; it can be attached to some verbs ending in *-it*, such as *exhibit(ion)*, *fruit(ion)*, *inhibit(ion)* and *prohibit(ion)*. Other verbs ending in *it* take *ssion*, as we shall soon see.

There are several verbs ending in *ish* which do *not* take the suffix *-ition*; for example, *banish,* and *embellish* both take *ment* to form the nouns. *Furnish* forms *furniture* and *furnishing*, a present participle used as a noun.

The noun *condition*, by a back-formation, has given rise to a verb which is the same word.

I have already given examples of *-otion* nouns formed from *-ote* verbs (such as *devotion* from *devote*), but a notable exception is *denote*, which gives not "denotion" but *denotation*.

I have also given examples of *-ution* nouns formed from *-ute* verbs (such as *pollution* from *pollute*). *Diminution*, however, is not from a non-existent word "diminute" but from *diminish*. This verb should have led to "diminition", but some long-forgotten printer may have been nodding and unwittingly inaugurated a new spelling.

Dissolve gives two nouns—*dissolution* (of Parliament, for example) and *solution* (in chemistry). Other verbs ending in *olve*, with the *ve* replaced by *ution*, are: *absolve, absolution; devolve, devolution; evolve, evolution; resolve, resolution; revolve, revolution.* The usual noun from *involve* is *involvement*, but there is an archaic noun *involution*.

Despite the fact that most *-ute* verbs form *-ution* nouns (such as *comminution* from *comminute*), it is as well to remember in this computer age that the noun from the verb *compute* is not "compution" but *computation*. Similar constructions are: *depute, deputation; impute, imputation; refute, refutation.*

I have already dealt with the suffix *-sion* in *pretension* from *pretend* and similar constructions, but the suffix is applied also to some verbs ending in *ise*, with the *e* dropped, as in: *excise, excision; revise, revision; supervise, supervision. Televise* is not the verb from which *television* is derived, but is a back-formation —that is, the noun appeared before the verb.

There is an interesting group of verbs ending in *de* (preceded by a vowel) in which this ending is dropped and replaced by *sion* to form nouns. This is a large group, but I select the following examples: *collide, collision; conclude, conclusion; decide, decision; divide, division; evade, evasion; extrude, extrusion; invade, invasion; persuade, persuasion; provide, provision.*

The suffix *-sion* is also applied to some verbs ending in *rt*, when the *t* is dropped and replaced by *sion*. The following are examples: *avert, aversion; convert, conversion; divert, diversion; invert, inversion; revert, reversion.*

As well as *-sion* there is the double-*s* suffix *-ssion*, often occurring with verbs ending in *eed* or *ede*. There are, for example: *accede, accession; concede, concession; intercede, intercession; proceed, procession; secede, secession.* Yet *precede* gives not "precession" but *precedence*.

Now here is a warning. Many people fall down with *supersede*, understandably giving it a *c* instead of an *s*. The noun, too, is spelt with an *s*: *supersession*.

The suffix *-ssion* is also attracted by some verbs ending in *it*, such as: *emit, emission; omit, omission; transmit, transmission.*

Remit gives *remission,* but it also gives *remittance,* and the suffix *-ance* will be considered later.

To conclude our survey of the *-ion* suffix I shall deal with the series of nouns in which the suffix is preceded by a vowel and *ct* (*-action, -ection, -iction, -oction, -uction*). In some cases the vowel and *ct* form part of the basic verb itself, as in *protract(ion)* and *retract(ion).* In other cases the vowel and *ct* do not form part of the basic verb, which then suffers some amendment. I have already referred to *liquefy* (*liquefaction*) and *putrefy* (*putrefaction*). *Rarefy* gives both *rarefaction* and *rarefication,* but *satisfy* gives only *satisfaction.*

Following are examples of verbs ending in *ect, ict* and *oct* with corresponding nouns:

ect: *bisect(ion)*; *direct(ion)*; *dissect(ion)*; *protect(ion)*.

ict: *constrict(ion)*; *contradict(ion)*; *derelict(ion)*; *predict(ion)*; *restrict(ion)*.

oct: *concoct(ion)*; *decoct(ion)*.

Most of the verbs producing nouns ending in *uction* end in *e,* which is dropped to give, for example, the following: *deduce, deduction*; *induce, induction*; *produce, production*; *seduce, seduction.* (*Induce* produces another electrical noun, *inductance.*) *Conduct,* which does not end in *e,* leads to *conduction,* but there is also *conductivity.* *Abduct* (no final *e*) gives *abduction.* The peculiarity of *destroy* and *destruction* was considered earlier.

We have seen what happens to *adopt* and *adapt* when they are converted to nouns (page 35). Other verbs ending in *pt* behave like *adopt* in taking the suffix *-ion* without any amendments, as in *corrupt(ion), intercept(ion)* and *interrupt(ion).* *Concept* is a noun, not a verb, and the noun *conception* is from the verb *conceive.* There is no verb "percept", and *perception* is from the verb *perceive.* Similarly, *reception* is from *receive* and *deception* from *deceive.*

-ant, -ent

Compared with the suffixes *-ment* and *-ion* for converting verbs to nouns, consideration of which has taken much space, other suffixes for the same purpose are few in number. Among them are *-ant* and *-ent*, which justify only a brief mention.

The suffix *-ant* forms, (for example) the following: *celebrate, celebrant*; *coagulate, coagulant*; *confide, confidant* (not to be confused with the adjective *confident*); *depend, dependant* (not to be confused with the adjective *dependent*); *lubricate, lubricant*; *migrate, migrant*; *mutate, mutant*; *occupy, occupant*; *serve, servant.*

The suffix *-ent* forms (for example) the following: *adhere, adherent* (a different noun from *adhesion*); *antecede, antecedent*; *correspond, correspondent*; *deter, deterrent* (r doubled); *precede, precedent*; *preside, president*. Indirect *-ent* formations include *agent* (from *act*), *recipient* (from *receive*), and *student* (from *study*).

Both *-ant* and *-ent* suffixes can also be attached to verbs to form adjectives, and we shall consider this function later.

-ance, -ence

Nouns are formed from some verbs with the suffixes *-ance* and *-ence*, and weak spellers sometimes find difficulty in remembering which to use of the two. There is no absolute rule about this, and the existence of a final *e* has no bearing on the decision, as is obvious from the lists below. It will be appreciated that these words are merely examples and that there are, in fact, very many others ending in *-ance* or *-ence*.

-ance nouns: *verbs with final e*		*-ance nouns:* *verbs without final e*	
dominate	dominance	attend	attendance
grieve	grievance	clear	clearance
ignore	ignorance	convey	conveyance
reassure	reassurance	forbear	forbearance
remonstrate	remonstrance	inherit	inheritance
tolerate	tolerance	maintain	maintenance
		perform	performance
		remit	remittance

-ence nouns: verbs with final e		*-ence nouns:* verbs without final e	
adhere	adherence	abhor	abhorrence
coincide	coincidence	defer	deference
condole	condolence	excel	excellence
confide	confidence	infer	inference
precede	precedence	obey	obedience
subserve	subservience	refer	reference
subside	subsidence	subsist	subsistence

It is odd that the verb *obey* gives not "obeyence" or "obeyance" as a noun but *obedience*. If spelling were logical—and I am not complaining if it is illogical—it should at least correspond with *convey(ance)*. Another anomaly in the lists is the formation of *maintenance* (not "maintainance") from *maintain*. In *subservience* an unnecessary *i* has been inserted. In *abhorrence* the *r* is doubled, but in *deference, inference* and *reference* it remains single.

The suffixes *-ance* and *-ence* are also applied in the conversion of some adjectives to nouns.

-ism, -ysis, -asm

In this heading I have written *-ism* and *-ysis* for the sake of clarity. Strictly, the effective suffixes are *-m* and *-is*, but the word-endings to be considered are as above.

Although the ending *ism* is usually applied to adjectives and nouns it is also applied to some verbs in their conversion to nouns. For example, the verb *criticise* leads to the noun *criticism, dogmatise* to *dogmatism*, and *plagiarise* to *plagiarism*. In each case the final *e* is dropped and replaced simply by *m*.

The ending *ysis* is found mostly in the vocabulary of scientists. It is applied to verbs ending in *yse*, in which the *e* is dropped and replaced by *is*. For instance, the verb *analyse* leads to *analysis*, and *electrolyse* leads to *electrolysis*. In *synthesise*, when the *e* is dropped, there is no need for any replacement to give the noun *synthesis*.

I mention *-asm* only as an incidental opportunity to point out that *enthusiasm* is not derived from a verb "enthuse". This verb, used colloquially, is a back-formation from the noun.

-al

I have already remarked that *retirement* in England means the same as *retiral* in Scotland. It might be conjectured from this that other *-ment* words in England can alternatively take *-al* in Scotland, but I believe that *retire* is alone in this treatment.

Other examples of *-al* nouns from verbs include: *acquit, acquittal*; *arouse, arousal*; *avow, avowal*; *betray, betrayal*; *carouse, carousal*; *rebut, rebuttal*; *rehearse, rehearsal*; *withdraw, withdrawal*. It will be seen that where the basic verb ends in *e* the *e* is dropped, and where it ends in *t* the *t* is doubled. *Rebut* can also form *rebutment*.

Most verbs ending in *ate* are converted to nouns by the use of such suffixes as *-ment* and *-ion*. An example of the rare use of *-al* with a verb ending in *ate* is *reciprocal* (as a noun) from *reciprocate*.

It may seem confusing that verbs similar to those mentioned, when converted to nouns, take not *-al* but some other suffix. For example, although *withdraw* takes *-al* to form *withdrawal*, *draw* takes *-ing* to form *drawing*. In spite of *arousal* and *carousal* there are *sousing* and *delousing*. In spite of *betrayal* there are *playing* and *payment*.

The suffix *-al* can also form adjectives.

-age

The suffix *-age* is generally attached to nouns, but in a few cases it is attached to verbs. The geological term *cleavage*, for example, comes from the basic verb *cleave* (with the final *e* dropped). *Usage* (a noun often employed by writers on language) may be from the verb or noun *use*, again with the *e* dropped. *Waste* and *post*, too, can be regarded either as verbs or nouns in their conversion to *wastage* and *postage*.

There are modernisms, manufactured from verbs for the sake of convenience, such as *coverage* and *reportage*. When the introduction of such words into the language arises out of necessity their use cannot be condemned, for nearly all words have appeared from necessity at some time or other. Legitimate reasons for condemnation include confusion of structure (for example, mixture of roots) and lack of euphony.

Some users of the suffix *-age* show remarkable ingenuity. I once saw an invoice on which the various additions to the basic amount—sales tax, allowance for inflation and other charges—were entered as "total plussage".

The suffix *-age* is found more frequently in French than in English, perhaps because in its pronunciation it comes easily to the tongue.

-ry, -ery

A few verbs are converted to nouns by the suffix *-ry* to result, for example, in *bake(ry)*, *husband(ry)*, *mimic(ry)*, *outlaw(ry)* and *revel(ry)*. (Here, *husband* is the verb "to manage or cultivate", and *outlaw* is in its verbal sense.) In some cases *e* precedes the *ry* to give words like *brew(ery)*, *hatch(ery)* and *wash(ery)*. In the case of *launder* the *e* is dropped to give *laundry*. These two suffixes are usually attached to nouns, however, as I shall show later.

-ure

The suffix *-ure* is used for converting a few verbs to nouns. If the basic verb ends in a consonant the suffix is a simple addition, as in *fail(ure)*. Similarly, *forfeit*, which is both noun and verb, gives *forfeit(ure)*. In *proceed* there is slight modification to form *procedure*. There is also modification in the conversion of *invest* to *investiture*, where *it* has been inserted, unnecessarily. (The word does not mean the same as *investment*.)

If the verb ends in *e* this is dropped, as in: *erase, erasure; legislate, legislature; pose, posture* (with *t* inserted); *seize, seizure*. In the case of *ligature* there is a verb *ligate*, which, however, I suspect to be a back-formation. Another back-formation is a verb *sculpt* from the noun *sculpture*. The formation of *furniture* from *furnish* was mentioned earlier.

The suffix *-ure* is applied to a few adjectives but usually to nouns, and I shall consider it again later.

-acy

Some verbs can be converted into nouns by the use of *-acy*, with slight alteration to the ending of the original. Thus, from the verb *conspire* the noun is *conspiracy*, and from *advocate* the noun is *advocacy*. The suffix is also attached to nouns and adjectives, and these uses will receive our attention at the appropriate times.

-er, -ster

Laughter, a noun in a class by itself, is more likely to come from the verb *laugh* than from the noun, but whatever the origin the result is the same. The suffix *-er*, however, is used in an "action" or "occupation" sense as explained in the next section.

The suffix *-ster* is usually attached to adjectives or nouns, but an example of its use with a verb is *spinster*. I wonder, incidentally, why it was once apparently assumed that only unmarried ladies did the spinning.

"Action" suffixes

Several suffixes are used to describe the actions or occupations of people or the uses of things. Most of them are added to nouns, but some are added to verbs, sometimes with slight alterations to the verb-endings. The suffixes generally in use are *-er*, *-or*, *-ant* and *-ist* (or *-yst*), and there is the rarer *-ar*. Where the *-ist* suffix is used with a verb ending in *ise* the real suffix is *-t*, the final *e* being dropped. There are several inconsistencies in the application of these suffixes, and the commonest cause of doubt is the choice between *er* and *or*.

I have called such suffixes "action" suffixes for the sake of convenience, and examples of their applications are given in the lists below. The verbs selected, of course, are only a few out of hundreds.

Verb	Related noun	Verb	Related noun
-er		*-or*	
betray	betrayer	act	actor
buy	buyer	convey	conveyor
carry	carrier	decorate	decorator
cool	cooler	distribute	distributor
defend	defender	lease	lessor
haul	haulier	mediate	mediator
inform	informer	pave	pavior (paviour)
magnify	magnifier	purvey	purveyor
plaster	plasterer	sail	sailor
send	sender	survey	surveyor
spell	speller	vend	vendor
upholster	upholsterer		
write	writer		

Verb -ant	Related noun	Verb -ist, -yst	Related noun
aspire	aspirant	anaesthetise	anaesthetist
celebrate	celebrant	analyse	analyst
coagulate	coagulant	apologise	apologist
cool	coolant	catalyse	catalyst
defend	defendant	dogmatise	dogmatist
defoliate	defoliant	dramatise	dramatist
depend	dependant	pacify	pacifist
enter	entrant	plagiarise	plagiarist
inform	informant		
inhabit	inhabitant	*-ar*	
pollute	pollutant	beg	beggar
		lie	liar

Some examples from these lists demand attention. It is curious, for instance, that, although *send* leads to *sender*, *vend* leads to *vendor*. There is no logical reason why *haulier* and *pavior* (or *paviour*) should have an *i* inserted, and there is no apparent justification for *lessor* instead of "leasor". A near parallel to *pavior* (or *paviour*) is *saviour* from the verb *save*; in American English the noun is *savior*, but *Saviour* is retained in the Christian sense.

The verb *inform* is deliberately given two places in the lists, because an *informer*, with its forensic connotation, is not the same as *informant*. The verb *cool* also is given two places; a *cooler* is usually understood as a place into which something is put to be cooled, and a *coolant* is a medium (a liquid, for instance) which circulates around something (such as machinery) to keep it cool. The duplication of *defend* is justified because a *defender* supports the interests of a *defendant*.

I have excluded from the *-ant* list the verb *confide* and the noun *confidant*. A *confidant* (contrary to the opinion of some misusers of the word) is not the person who confides but the person who receives the confidential information.

A *dependant* (noun) is a person who *depends* (verb) on someone else and is therefore *dependent* (adjective) on him.

To include *burglar* and *pedlar* in the short *-ar* list would not be strictly legitimate, as these nouns appeared before the verbs *burgle* and *peddle* which are thus back-formations.

Verbs ending in *y* are not consistent in their behaviour. Thus, although *magnify* leads to *magnifier*, *pacify* leads to *pacifist*. A minor irregularity is observed in the treatment of the verb *enter*, which perhaps should give the noun "enterant", but tradition has reduced the word to *entrant*.

The connection of action suffixes with nouns will be considered later.

-ing

Very often the present participle of a verb is used as a noun ending in the suffix *-ing*. For example, the following are legitimate: "The *giving* of donations is welcome" (as an alternative to *gift*); "From the *rising* of the sun . . ."; "His *comings* and *goings* are difficult to trace"; "As a leader he has a tremendous *following*".

-ee, -and

The suffix *-ee* is a relic of the French suffix *é* (masculine) or *ée* (feminine). Originally it was adopted in English in the same form, but gradually the acute accent was dropped and *ee* retained to cover both sexes. The following are examples of its use: *address, addressee*; *employ, employee*; *lease* (as verb), *lessee* (the other party being the *lessor*); *pay, payee*; *vend, vendee* (the party at the selling end being the *vendor*). Occasionally you find the meanings reversed, particularly with the two nouns derived from the verb *mortgage*. The party who lends money on the security of an estate is the *mortgagee*; the borrowing party is the *mortgagor* (or, less commonly, *mortgager*).

A beneficiary under a will is a *legatee*, and although this is derived from a verb *legate* the verb has largely fallen into disuse in favour of *bequeath*.

The suffix *-and* is of limited application. An undergraduate about to receive his degree, and thus become a graduate, is a *graduand*. An aspiring clerk in holy orders offering himself for ordination is an *ordinand*.

CONVERSION OF VERBS TO ADJECTIVES

Verbs are converted to adjectives by the addition of suffixes which may or may not require some alteration to the ending of the basic verb. These suffixes include the following: *-able, -ible*; *-ous*; *-ory*; *-ive*; *-al*; *-ant, -ent*; *-some, -ful*.

-able, -ible

These two suffixes, applied to some verbs and some nouns to make adjectives, give rise to confusion even in newspapers. The following are *general* rules.

Some verbs ending in consonants take *able* without any alteration, as in: *accept(able), book(able)* ("All seats are bookable"), *comfort(able), favour(able)* and *honour(able). Explain* should lead to "explainable", but there is no such word. The derived adjective is *explicable*, from a basic verb *explicate* which means the same as *explain* but is never used.

If the basic verb ends in *ate* this ending is dropped and replaced by *able*. Common results of this treatment include: *abominate, abominable*; *appreciate, appreciable*; *calculate, calculable*; *demonstrate, demonstrable*; *educate, educable*; *irritate, irritable.*

If the basic verb ends in *e* after a consonant (or after *s*) the *e* is usually dropped, to give, for example: *admire, admirable*; *debate, debatable*; *prove, provable*; *use, usable.* Although *movable* is standard, *moveable* is sometimes accepted. *Despise* should make "despisable", but the adjective is *despicable.*

If the basic verb ends in *ce* the *e* is retained, as in *enforce(able), pronounce(able)* and *trace(able).*

Words ending in *age* are usually nouns, some of which attract the suffix *-able* to form adjectives, and I shall deal with these later. There are also a few verbs ending in *age* which take *-able*, and in these the final *e* is usually retained, as in *assuage(able), damage(able)* and *manage(able). Damage*, of course, is also a noun.

If the basic verb ends in *y* after a consonant, the *y* is replaced by *i*, as in: *descry, descriable*; *pity, pitiable*; *rely, reliable.* This rule, as usual, can break down. *Apply*, for example, should make "appliable" (which I have seen), but the adjective, used every day, is *applicable*. *Friable*, incidentally, has no connection with the verb *fry*; it is a scientific term meaning "easily crumbled". *Viable* ("practicable" in its commonest modern sense) has nothing to do with *vie* ("to rival, compete with").

If the basic verb ends in *y* after a vowel, the *y* is retained. There are few words of this kind, examples being *assay(able)*, *convey(able)*, *pay(able)* and *play(able)*.

There is an opportunity here to talk about the vexed adjective *inflammable*, which is derived from the basic verb *inflame* (with the *e* dropped and the *m* doubled). Unfortunately, the prefix *in-* can easily be regarded as *not*, to result in a complete misinterpretation of the word as "not liable to burst into flame" and therefore "safe". Confusion is now sometimes avoided by using the word *flammable* to convey the correct meaning.

The suffix *-ible* seems to be more attracted to nouns than to verbs, and the number of verbs taking this suffix is limited. Some of them end in *e*, in which case the *e* is dropped to give, for example: *collapse, collapsible*; *force, forcible*; *reverse, reversible*.

In some cases, if the basic verb ends in *t* or *d*, the last letter is dropped and replaced by *sible* or *ssible*. For example, *comprehend* makes *comprehensible*, *defend* makes *defensible*, and *reprehend* makes *reprehensible*. Use of the double *s* is exemplified by *admissible* (from *admit*), *omissible* (from *omit*) and *permissible* (from *permit*). Exceptions from this practice include *controvert(ible)* and *resist(ible)*, where the suffix is simply added to the basic verb without any alteration.

In cases where the basic verb ends in a consonant other than *t* or *d*, the suffix is again simply added to the base, as in *discern(ible)* and *gull(ible)*.

I shall deal with the adjectives *contemptible* and *contemptuous* under noun-adjective conversions rather than verb-adjective conversions, as these adjectives are derived from the noun *contempt* and not directly from the verb *contemn*.

Irregularities are not hard to find. Thus, *neglect* makes not "neglectible" but *negligible*, and it may not be generally known, as a similarity, that *eligible* comes from the verb *elect*.

The verb *eat* makes use of both suffixes to give *eatable* and *edible*.

Although the verb *reduce* ends in *ce* it takes not *able* but *ible*, with the final *e* dropped, to give *reducible*.

The adjective *practicable*, though related to the noun *practice* and the verb *practise*, is not directly derived from either, and cannot readily be accommodated in any of the word-groups we have been considering. It should be remembered that it does not mean quite the same as *practical*, which, however, is sometimes used when *practicable* would be more suitable. (See "Notes on Selected Words".)

It may seem anomalous that although *resolve* makes *resolvable* the similar verb *dissolve* makes not "dissolvable" but *dissoluble*. This means virtually the same as *soluble*, which is used in chemistry. (It is of incidental interest that *resolvable* has an archaic form, now never used, *resoluble*.) We shall be examining negative forms of words later, but it is appropriate here to point out that both *dissoluble* and *soluble* take the negative prefix *in-* to make *indissoluble* and *insoluble*.

Legitimate attempts have been made to differentiate between the use of *-able* and *-ible* on etymological grounds, but the attempts have partly broken down in the face of established tradition. Tradition may have been influenced by carelessness, but sometimes consistency may have been sacrificed to the more pleasant sound or attractive appearance of a word. The conclusion seems to be that the "correct" choice between *-able* and *-ible* depends less on rules than on a good visual memory, and for the benefit of the reader I shall give later in the book lists of some fairly common *-able* and *-ible* adjectives made from verbs and nouns.

-ous

A few verbs (not many) can be converted to adjectives by the suffix *-ous*. We have already seen (page 34) how the verb *pretend* can form three nouns, one of which, *pretentiousness*, is an extension of the derived adjective *pretentious* (that is, derived from *pretence*). Most *-ous* adjectives, in fact, are made from nouns, as will be discussed on page 60.

One of the verbs taking *-ous* is *ponder*, which, originally meaning "to weigh carefully in the mind", has gradually come to be applied to deep thought generally and so given rise to the adjective *ponderous*. An irregularity is immediately evident, however, when it is realised that *wonder* (as a verb), though similar to *ponder*, does not make "wonderous" but *wondrous* (without an *e*).

A similar construction is seen in *cumbrous*, from *cumber* (an early form of *encumber*), for which another adjective is *cumbersome*. The noun *disaster* follows the same pattern, leading to *disastrous* (not "disasterous", a spelling of which even some journalists are guilty). The adjective *piteous* is derived from *pity*, which can be a noun or a verb, the *y* having been replaced by *e*. (A note on the misused *pity* adjectives will be found on page 129).

The verb *tremble* should perhaps form an easy adjective "tremblous", but its adjective is *tremulous*, which sounds more pleasant. A similar treatment is given to the verb *bib* (to tipple, as in "wine-bibber"), of which the adjective is *bibulous*.

-ory

The suffix *-ory* can be applied to some verbs and some nouns. Applied to verbs, it is usually, but not always, part of *-atory*, as in: *declaim, declamatory*; *exclaim, exclamatory*; *explain, explanatory*; *retaliate, retaliatory*. It is seen from these words that where there is *ai* the *i* is dropped, and where the verb ends in *e* this is dropped.

A verb needing no alteration before the suffix is *inhibit*, which makes *inhibitory*. *Compel* needs modification to make *compulsory*. It might be thought that *repel*, a similar verb to *compel*, should make "repulsory", but the adjective is *repellent*, which is also a noun. (The suffixes *-ant* and *-ent* are discussed later.) In *promise* the *e* is dropped to form *promissory*.

There is strange inconsistency with verbs ending in *ide*. Consider three rather similar verbs: *decide, divide* and *deride*. *Decide* makes the adjective *decisive*, *divide* makes *divisive*, and only *deride* nicely fits into this section with its adjective *derisory*.

-ive

There are many verbs which can be converted to adjectives by the suffix *-ive*. Where the basic verb ends in *e* the *e* is dropped to give, for example, the following: *cumulate* (an archaic form of *accumulate*), *cumulative*; *cure, curative*; *decorate, decorative*;

indicate, indicative; *restore, restorative*; *speculate, speculative*. Irregularities, where *d* is replaced by *s*, include: *conclude, conclusive*; *decide, decisive*; *divide, divisive*; *exclude, exclusive*; *include, inclusive*.

Two of the verbs ending in *ke* (mentioned on page 35 in connection with the conversion of verbs to nouns), *evoke* and *provoke*, can also be converted to adjectives with the aid of the suffix *-ive*. The *e* is dropped, but in addition the *k*, strangely, is replaced by the hard *c* to give *evocative* and *provocative*. Although the verbs *invoke* and *revoke* are similar to the two just cited, they do not make *-ive* adjectives but *invocable* and *revocable*.

Where the basic verb ends in a consonant the suffix is simply added, in such cases, for example, as *construct(ive), express(ive), instruct(ive), possess(ive)* and *prevent(ive)*. "Preventative", referred to elsewhere in this book, is to be discouraged as the repetition of the *t* makes the word less euphonious than *preventive*, and yet *represent(ative)* has only one form. The suffix is legitimately extended to *-ative* in *affirm(ative)* and *confirm(ative)*, but no repetition of *t* is involved.

The *-ative* adjectives listed in the first paragraph of this section are derived from verbs which themselves end in *ate*. *Conserve* and *preserve*, however, which do not end in *ate*, also form *-ative* adjectives (and nouns)—*conservative* and *preservative*. Two other *-erve* verbs take different suffixes to make adjectives, the adjective from *deserve* being the present participle *deserving* and the adjective from *reserve* the past participle *reserved*.

Other cases concern verbs ending in *end*, in which the *d* is replaced by *sive* to give the following: *apprehend, apprehensive*; *comprehend, comprehensive*; *defend, defensive*; *offend, offensive*. (*Defensive* and *offensive* are also nouns.) The suffix *-ive* is also taken by some verbs ending in *it*, the *t* being replaced by *ss* to form: *admit, admissive*; *permit, permissive*; *submit, submissive*. The first two examples do not mean the same as the other related adjectives *admissible* and *permissible*.

-al

We have already examined the conversion of verbs to nouns by the suffix *-al*, and the suffix can also be used to convert verbs to adjectives. I have pointed out that *practical* (as well as *practicable*) is associated with, but not directly derived from, the noun *practice* and the verb *practise*. Other adjectives formed with *-al*, which *are* directly derived from verbs, include the following: *criticise, critical*; *equivocate, equivocal*; *pontificate, pontifical*. The suffix is more commonly used in the conversion of nouns to adjectives, however, and this use will be considered later.

-ant, -ent

We have seen how the suffixes *-ant* and *-ent* can be used to convert some verbs into related nouns, and the same suffixes can be used in the formation of some adjectives. Some adjectives are formed from nouns ending in *-ance* and *-ence*, but it cannot be concluded that all the derived nouns listed on page 40 can automatically be changed into adjectives by the replacement of *-ance* or *-ence* by *-ant* or *-ent*. Of the derived nouns listed, only the following (in alphabetical order) make *-ant* or *-ent* adjectives:

Noun	Adjective	Noun	Adjective
abhorrence	abhorrent	ignorance	ignorant
adherence	adherent	obedience	obedient
attendance	attendant	precedence	precedent
coincidence	coincident	subservience	subservient
confidence	confident	subsistence	subsistent
dominance	dominant	tolerance	tolerant
excellence	excellent		

Other *-ant* adjectives (besides those mentioned above) are: *defy, defiant*; *please, pleasant*; *repent, repentant*; *vibrate, vibrant*. Some are independent of verbs, such as *adamant, brilliant* and *constant*. (*Adamant* was originally a noun meaning *diamond*.)

Adjectives ending in *-ent* made from verbs are commoner. Besides those already mentioned there are: *decay, decadent*; *deliquesce, deliquescent*; *effervesce, effervescent*; and others. The adjective *confident* (having confidence in something or someone) is different from the adjective *confidential* (secret, not to be disclosed). *Coincidental* is merely a longer form of *coincident*.

Included in the list on page 41 are the three similar verbs

defer, infer and *refer*, which form the nouns *deference, inference* and *reference*. These nouns, however, do not lead to *-ent* adjectives but to *deferential, inferential* and *referential*.

-some, -ful

There are several adjectives ending in *-some*, but not all are derived from verbs. One is *cumbersome*, noted earlier as an alternative to *cumbrous*, which is derived from the verb *cumber* (or *encumber*). Others derived from verbs are *fear(some), grue(some), quarrel(some), tire(some)* and *win(some)*. There are *-some* adjectives derived from nouns and others derived from other adjectives. Some of these, which have been with us for centuries, have the respectability of age; others of more modern origin sound artificial.

The following is a list of *-some* adjectives which are not derived from verbs but are included here for want of a suitable place elsewhere: *awesome, fulsome, gladsome, handsome, lightsome, lonesome, wholesome*. As a matter of interest, *gruesome* is from a verb *grue* which means "to shudder, to feel horror or dread".

Although the suffix *-ful* is attached to many nouns to form adjectives and other nouns, it is attracted by few verbs. One is *mourn*, which makes *mournful*. *Vengeful* is related to *revenge* (verb and noun) and to *vengeance* (noun).

CONVERSION OF ADJECTIVES TO NOUNS

Adjectives are converted to nouns by use of the following suffixes: *-ness*; *-ity*; *-ion*; *-acy*; *-ery, ry*; *-ment*; *-ism*; *-ance, -ancy*; *-ence, -ency*; *-escence* (an expansion of *-ence*); *-iety*. These will be considered in turn.

-ness

Most adjectives can be converted into nouns by the straightforward addition of the suffix *-ness*. To give examples would be unnecessary were it not for the opportunity to make several observations and point out exceptions.

Adjectives ending in *y* have the *y* replaced by *i* to give, for example, *beastliness, happiness, saintliness* and *sprightliness*. The adjective *busy* follows the same rule; its derived noun, *business*, is now hardly ever, if at all, connected with the adjective, being used as an isolated noun in itself.

It is possible to form two separate nouns from the same base. For example, there are *persuasiveness* and *persuasion*, but they have different meanings, the first being from the adjective *persuasive* and the second from the verb *persuade*. The verb *consider* gives *consideration*, while the adjective *considerate* gives *considerateness*. *Faithful* gives *faithfulness*, but it also gives *fidelity* which means the same.

-ity

Fidelity, from the Latin form of the adjective *faithful*, brings us to the suffix *-ity*. Where the adjective does not end in *e*, the *ity* is normally a straightforward appendage, as in *fluid(ity)*, *humid(ity)*, *infirm(ity)*, *morbid(ity)* and *senior(ity)*. In the treatment of most nouns ending in *l* the *l* remains single, as in *jovial(ity)*, *normal(ity)* and *plural(ity)*. An exception is *tranquil*, where the *l* is doubled to give *tranquillity*.

Irregular, of course, leads to *irregularity*, and we find an irregularity in the conversion of the adjective *profound* to the noun *profundity*, where the *o* is lost. *Odd* forms *oddness* and *oddity*, the first being a general state of being odd and the second a particular peculiarity. It is strange that while the noun *longevity* is in fairly common use, the adjective from which it is derived, *longeval*, meaning long-lived, is hardly ever heard.

Where the basic adjective ends in *e* the *e* is dropped, as in the following examples: *agile, agility*; *diverse, diversity*; *ductile, ductility*; *infinite, infinity*; *profane, profanity*; *pure, purity*; *senile, senility*; *suave, suavity*. *Crude* and *nude*, by the same rule, make *crudity* and *nudity*, but tantalisingly *rude* makes not "rudity" but *rudeness*.

There is the rather long process by which the original basic verb is converted to an *-able* or *-ible* adjective which in turn is converted to a noun ending in the suffix *-ity*. In such cases the final *le* is dropped before replacement by the suffix. Examples are innumerable (this word would give *innumerability*), and rather than give examples here I refer the reader to the list of *-able* and *-ible* adjectives, made from verbs and nouns, on page 96.

Interpolation: adjectives ending in ous

Where an adjective ends in *ous* it *may* be derived from the noun but not necessarily. I am sure that the adjective *monstrous* (with *u*) appeared before the noun *monstrosity* (without *u*), *curious* before *curiosity*, *ferocious* before *ferocity*, and *porous* before *porosity*, and that in the formation of the nouns the *u* was dropped for convenience. On the other hand there are instances where the noun probably appeared before the *-ous* adjective; for example, *fury* probably came before *furious* and *parsimony* before *parsimonious*.

I am giving the following *-ous* adjectives the benefit of any doubt and assuming that they appeared before their corresponding nouns: *ambiguous, ambiguity*; *ambitious, ambition, ambitiousness* (not quite the same as *ambition*); *devious, deviousness* (not the same as *deviation*); *fortuitous, fortuity*; *hilarious, hilarity*; *ingenious, ingenuity*; *ingenuous, ingenuousness*. (It is fortuitous that the similar adjectives *ingenious* and *ingenuous* make different noun-forms, as otherwise they would be even less understood than they are.) Another adjective which makes two different nouns is *precocious*, which leads to *precociousness* and *precocity*.

-ion

Although, as we have seen, there are many verbs which can be converted to nouns by the suffix *-ion*, the direct process is applied to only a few adjectives. For example, *abject* gives *abjection* and *contrite* gives *contrition*. The noun *discretion* is from the adjective *discreet*, but there is also an adjective *discrete*, which means "distinct, discontinuous, detached, separate", the noun from which is *discreteness*.

The *-ion* suffix is also part of the involved process seen in the formation of words like *resolution*. This began as a verb, *resolve*, which led to an adjective, *resolute*, which in turn led to the noun *resolution*. The adjective and noun derived from *dissolve* (mentioned on page 38), however,—*dissolute* and *dissolution*—have connections far removed from the scientific sense of *dissolve*. The verbs *devolve, evolve* and *revolve* miss the intermediate adjectival stage to result in the nouns *devolution, evolution* and *revolution*, but these can be carried a step further and form the adjectives *devolutionary, evolutionary* and *revolutionary*.

-acy

The suffix *-acy* can be applied to adjectives and verbs to form nouns and to nouns to form other nouns. For the present, however, we are concerned with the conversion of adjectives. We may be on delicate ground here, for in some instances it is questionable which came first, the adjective or the noun.

Diplomacy perhaps preceded *diplomatic*, and *fallacy* could have been on the scene before *fallacious*. In other cases, however, there is no doubt that the adjective came first, examples of these being: *accurate, accuracy*; *delicate, delicacy*; *obstinate, obstinacy*; *profligate, profligacy*; *supreme, supremacy*.

-ery, -ry

The suffixes *-ery* and *-ry*, which we have already seen in their association with verbs, can also be used occasionally in the conversion of adjectives to nouns. Examples are *bravery* from *brave* and *greenery* from *green*. The suffix *-ry* can also be used to convert nouns to other nouns, as we shall see later.

-ment

The suffix *-ment* readily attaches itself to verbs to form nouns but is not greatly attracted to adjectives. The adjective *merry* forms the noun *merriment*, but some dictionaries allow *merriness* to exist.

Another example of the use of *-ment* in the conversion of adjectives to nouns is in *betterment*, but a note of caution is necessary. *Better* is an adjective of comparison ("good, better, best"), and hence conversion to the noun *betterment* seems legitimate. The word is almost invariably applied to property, however, in the sense of "improvement", and I suspect that *betterment* is derived not from the adjective but from a back-formation verb *to better.*

-ism

Apart from its use in converting nouns to other nouns (to be considered later) and verbs to nouns (page 41), the suffix *-ism* is used in several cases for converting adjectives to nouns. Some of the *-ism* nouns thus formed are names of practices, theories, cults and attitudes, but others are more ordinary nouns. In many cases the suffix is a simple appendage to the basic adjective, but in others modification is required. The following examples include both kinds: *altruistic, altruism; American(ism); archaic, archaism; colloquial(ism); didactic(ism); monetary, monetarism; mystic(ism); spiritual(ism); true, truism; witty, witticism.*

There are inconsistencies. If *didactic* and *mystic* make *didacticism* and *mysticism* why do not *altruistic* and *archaic* make "altruisticism" and "archaicism"? In the formation of *witticism* the adjective *witty* has been treated as if it were "wittic".

-ance, -ancy, -ence, -ency

In the conversion of some adjectives to nouns these four suffixes are common, *-ance* and *-ancy* replacing *-ant* and *-ence* and *-ency* replacing *-ent*. Weak spellers often find difficulty in deciding whether to use *a* or *e*, but, as in many other spelling problems, a good visual memory helps. The following are short lists of typical conversions.

Adjective	Noun	Adjective	Noun
-ant to *-ance*		*-ant* to *-ancy*	
abundant	abundance	constant	constancy
attendant	attendance	expectant	expectancy
clairvoyant	clairvoyance	hesitant	hesitancy
dominant	dominance	infant	infancy
elegant	elegance	vacant	vacancy
fragrant	fragrance		
relevant	relevance		

Adjective	Noun	Adjective	Noun
-ent to *-ence*		*-ent* to *-ency*	
corpulent	corpulence	absorbent	absorbency
prominent	prominence	clement	clemency
reticent	reticence	consistent	consistency
subsistent	subsistence	fervent	fervency
		fluent	fluency
		strident	stridency

A few observations are necessary, for there is a certain laxity about some words of this kind. For example, *attendant, clairvoyant* and *infant* can be nouns as well as adjectives. There is a noun *ascendant* used, for example, in astronomy, but there are two adjectives, *ascendant* and *ascendent*, which are interchangeable and form both *ascendancy* and *ascendency*. *Brilliant* forms both *brilliance* and *brilliancy*, *eminent* both *eminence* and *eminency*, and *repellent* both *repellence* and *repellency*. (For a note on *dependent* and *dependant*, see page 117.)

-escence

A group of attractive words which could be placed in the "*-ent* to *-ence*" series is that in which adjectives ending in *escent* form nouns ending in *escence*, the adjectives themselves being in most cases derived from verbs. A list of examples follows.

Verb	Adjective	Noun
acquiesce	acquiescent	acquiescence
coalesce	coalescent	coalescence
convalesce	convalescent	convalescence
deliquesce	deliquescent	deliquescence
effervesce	effervescent	effervescence
evanesce	evanescent	evanescence
fluoresce	fluorescent	fluorescence
	iridescent	iridescence
	obsolescent	obsolescence
opalesce	opalescent	opalescence
phosphoresce	phosphorescent	phosphorescence
recrudesce	recrudescent	recrudescence
	senescent	senescence

Where no verb is shown, a verb does not exist.

-iety

A little-used suffix for converting adjectives to nouns is *-iety*, which gives, for example, the following: *anxious, anxiety*; *dubious, dubiety*; *pious, piety*; *proper, propriety*; *sober, sobriety*; *various, variety*.

Other adjective-noun suffixes

There are several other suffixes by which adjectives can be converted to nouns, some by means of simple appendage and others by modification of the basic word. Thus, *false* makes three nouns by the use of different suffixes, all with different meanings. The suffixes *-hood* and *-ness* are added to *false* to give *falsehood* and *falseness*, but in the case of *falsity* the *e* is dropped. The suffix *-hood* is usually applied to nouns, and examples will be given later.

Also applied to nouns is the suffix *-dom*, but it, too, can be applied to adjectives, as in the product *wisdom* from *wise,* the *e* being dropped. The suffix *-ship* is usually applied to nouns, but one adjective, *hard*, gives *hardship*. The addition of *-ster* to form nouns like *youngster* has little to recommend it except in certain cases, and the practice sounds somewhat contrived. I shall say no more about it here, as most of the *-ster* words are formed from nouns.

The suffix *-ure*, used mainly for converting verbs to nouns and nouns to other nouns, is used also for converting a few adjectives to nouns. One example is *rapture*, a noun formed from the adjective *rapt*. There is an obvious connection between the noun *literature* and the adjective *literate*, but evidence of actual conversion is lacking.

CONVERSION OF NOUNS TO ADJECTIVES

There are many ways of carrying out the reverse of the last process—instead of converting adjectives to nouns, converting nouns to adjectives. We have examined the delicate question of deciding which came first, and in the following notes I have tried to concentrate on examples in which the noun preceded the adjective so that the adjective was genuinely formed from the noun.

The suffixes to be considered are : *-y, -ly*; *-ish*; *-ous*; *-ic, -ics, -ical*; *-ary*; *-ar*; *-ful*; *-less*; *-al, -ial, -eal*; *-ate*; *-ine*; *-ian, -ean, -ese*; *-en*; *-esque*; *-able, -ible*; *-ose*; *-iac.*

-y, -ly

The simplest method of conversion in the numerous cases where the noun does not end in *e* is that of adding *y* to the noun to give, for example, *greed(y), meat(y), rubber(y)* and *weight(y)*—the list is almost endless.

If the basic noun ends in *e* the *e* is dropped before the *y*, to give, for example, the following: *haze, hazy*; *lace, lacy*; *sauce, saucy*; *shale, shaly*; *treacle, treacly.* The word *clay* is awkward as it ends in *y*, but the accepted geological adjective is *clayey* with an *e* inserted. *Day* could hardly give "dayey", however, and so its adjective (as described below) is *daily*.

A variation of the *-y* suffix in the formation of adjectives is *-ly*, which is attracted to some nouns in the sense of "having the quality of". Examples are *beast(ly), curmudgeon(ly), friend(ly), king(ly), mother(ly)* and *rascal(ly)*. Still as an adjectival suffix it is applied to nouns to give a sense of "at regular intervals", such as *hourly, daily* and *weekly*.

The adjectival use of *-ly* is not to be confused with its adverbial use, to which I shall refer later.

-ish

Another suffix for noun-adjective conversion is *-ish*, which in most cases is simply added to the basic noun, as in *book(ish), boy(ish), fever(ish)* and *fiend(ish)*. In the case of nouns ending in *e* practice varies; for example, both *rogueish* and *roguish* are acceptable. The suffix is also attached to adjectives to form other adjectives in the sense of "not quite", as in *reddish, smallish* and *youngish*. There are also adjectives derived from no particular nouns, such as *outlandish*. Most commonly, of course, the suffix is applied to nationality, as in *British, Polish* and *Spanish*, and to language.

-ous

The suffix *-ous*, already noted as an agent for converting verbs to adjectives and adjectives to nouns, can also be used for converting nouns to adjectives. Here again, in the simplest cases, the suffix is added to the basic noun to give, for example, *bulb(ous)*, *cretin(ous)*, *peril(ous)*, *poison(ous)* and *portent(ous)*.

If the basic noun ends in *y* the *y* is dropped and replaced by *ous*, *ious* or *eous*, as in the following: *anomaly*, *amomalous*; *calamity*, *calamitous*; *glory*, *glorious*; *parsimony*, *parsimonious*; *pity*, *piteous*. *Pity*, it is important to remember, gives three different adjectives, the other two being *pitiful* and *pitiable*, and for further discussion the reader is referred to page 129. *Beauty*, which ends in *y*, gives *beauteous* as an adjective as well as *beautiful*. *Atrocity* should form "atrocitous", but the adjective is *atrocious*. *Efficacy* should form "efficacous", but for smoothness an *i* has been inserted to make *efficacious*.

In the case of nouns ending in *our* the *u* is dropped before the *r* to give, for example, the following: *clamour*, *clamorous*; *dolour*, *dolorous*; *glamour*, *glamorous*; *humour*, *humorous*; *odour*, *odorous*; *tumour*, *tumorous*; *vapour*, *vaporous*. I remarked elsewhere that, in relation to the noun *amour*, there are two adjectives, *amorous* and *amatory*.

Two other nouns which need amendment before the suffix *-ous* are *number* and *mischief*. In *number* the *b* is dropped and *ous* added to give *numerous*. With *mischief*, the *f* is replaced by *v* to result in *mischievous*. Unfortunately in some parts of the British Isles the mispronunciation "mischievious" is heard.

In nouns ending in *er* the *e* is dropped in some cases and retained in others. With the *e* dropped we find the following: *disaster*, *disastrous*; *idolater*, *idolatrous*; *leper*, *leprous*; *monster*, *monstrous*; *wonder*, *wondrous*. With the *e* retained before the *r* we follow the practice already mentioned for the simplest cases and directly add the suffix to the basic noun, thereby reaching such words as *cancer(ous)*, *danger(ous)*, *murder(ous)*, *slander(ous)* and *thunder(ous)*. *Boisterous* and *obstreporous* are not related to any nouns. There is a reference to *ponderous* on page 50.

Where the noun ends in *ge* the *e* is retained and the suffix is a simple appendage, so that we find *courage(ous)* and *advantage(ous)*.

Nouns ending in *ce* take various suffixes to form adjectives, but, as far as *-ous* is concerned, the usual treatment is to replace the *e* by *ious* to give, for example: *avarice, avaricious*; *caprice, capricious*; *malice, malicious*; *space, spacious*; *vice, vicious*. The adjective from the noun *licence* is not "licencious" but *licentious*.

In nouns ending in *re* the *e* is dropped to give, for example: *adventure, adventurous*; *fibre, fibrous*; *lustre, lustrous*; *pore, porous*. An exception is *ochre*, the adjective from which is *ochreous*.

Nouns ending in vowels seldom take *-ous* to form adjectives, but when they do the construction is not simple. *Vertigo*, for example, could lead to a direct adjective "vertigous", but the adjective is the long *vertiginous*.

From the noun *tumult* the adjective should be "tumultous", but an extra *u* has been inserted to make it *tumultuous*. An extra *u* has similarly been inserted into *contemptuous* from the noun *contempt*. This adjective, incidentally, is different from *contemptible*, which applies to the person who, or the behaviour which, deserves the contemptuous person's contempt. Then there is the splendid adjective *tempestuous* from *tempest*.

The adjective from the noun *science* is *scientific*. Yet if we add *con* at the beginning, to make *conscience*, the adjective is not "conscientific" (which sounds horrible) but *conscientious*. *Contagion* (meaning contact) leads to *contagious*.

There are many *-ous* adjectives which are not related to nouns, or are related to nouns only by tenuous association or etymological connection. Such adjectives include *conspicuous, deciduous, horrendous, illustrious, scabrous, stupendous* and *tremendous*. Not included in this list are two interesting adjectives *dextrous* and *vicarious*, on which there are special notes on pages 117 and 137.

A few lines above I used the adjective *tenuous*. The associated noun is *tenuity*, but it is difficult to decide which appeared first. In the case of *pusillanimity* I think that this is the basic noun which gave rise to the adjective *pusillanimous*.

There are two extended *-ous* suffixes, *-iferous* and *-aceous*, the use of which is practically limited to science and technology. Adjectives incorporating these are either derived directly from nouns or have strong etymological connections. They include *arenaceous* (sandy), *carbonaceous* (carbon-bearing), *Carboniferous, Cretaceous, farinaceous* (floury) and *metalliferous* (associated with metals). The third and fourth words in this list are given capital initial letters as they are the names of geological periods.

There are also *-ous* adjectives derived from nouns which themselves are derived from verbs. For example, the verb *contend* leads to the noun *contention* which in turn leads to the adjective *contentious*. Similarly we find *presume, presumption* and *presumptuous* (*not* "presumptious").

From these many examples it is clear that "rules" for conversion of nouns into *-ous* adjectives apply only in *some* cases, so that in effect there are not any rules. There will be further necessary discussion of the suffix after the next section.

-ic, -ics, -ical

The suffix *-ic* for conversion of nouns to adjectives is found in many words. Where the basic noun ends in *e* the *e* is usually dropped, so that we find: *aesthete, aesthetic*; *athlete, athletic*; *metre, metric*; *oolite, oolitic*; *tone, tonic*. *Science, pedagogue* and *romance* happen to end in *e*, but the adjectives are *scientific, pedagogic* and *romantic*.

Where the basic noun ends in a consonant the suffix may be simply added, to give, for example, *alcohol(ic)*, *choler(ic)*, *lithograph(ic)*, *magnet(ic)* and *monotheist(ic)*. Exceptions include *horrific* from *horror*, *terrific* from *terror*, and *chaotic* from *chaos*.

Nouns ending in vowels other than *e* usually take the straightforward suffix to form adjectives without any modification, as in *algebra(ic)*, *delta(ic)* and *hero(ic)*. *Aroma* should give "aromaic", but the adjective is *aromatic*, just as the adjective from *dogma* is *dogmatic* and the adjective from *drama, dramatic*. The adjective from *giant* should be "giantic", but an unnecessary *g* has been inserted to make *gigantic*. (The adjective *pragmatic* is derived from a Latin word, and there is no English noun "pragma".)

With nouns ending in *y* the *y* is dropped and replaced by *ic* to give (for example) the following: *economy, economic*; *geography, geographic*; *geometry, geometric*; *harmony, harmonic*; *history, historic*; *melody, melodic*; *strategy, strategic*. Exceptions with nouns ending in *y* include: *fantasy, fantastic*; *poetry, poetic*; *tragedy, tragic. Biology* and *geology* attract the extended forms *biological* and *geological*.

Some *-ic* adjectives are derived from proper nouns, or names, and should not really be counted as legitimate words until they have become firmly established. By this I mean that *Byronic* and *Miltonic* (with capital initials) do not have the same status as *plutonic* (small *p*), a geological adjective applied to certain igneous rocks. *Hebrew* is an established proper noun giving the adjective *Hebraic. Mosaic*, applied to the Law of Moses, is not to be confused with the design of small stones called *mosaic*.

The suffix *-ic* is part of some adjectives that are not directly derived from nouns, such as *automatic, bucolic, comic, domestic, exotic* and *linguistic. Electric* is derived from the Greek word for amber, *elektron*, the ancient Greeks having discovered that if amber is rubbed it produces static electricity.

Applied to some special studies the suffix *-ic* is pluralised, as in the nouns *acoustics, economics, ethics, logistics, mathematics, physics* and *politics*. Adjectives formed from some of these pluralised nouns drop the *s* and extend the *-ic* suffix to *-ical*, giving, for example: *acoustical, ethical, mathematical, physical* and *political. Economical* has a sense of its own (thrifty) not necessarily directly connected with the study of economics. There is no accepted adjective "logistical", the usual word being *logistic*.

The suffix *-ical* can also be applied to some adjectives already attracting *-ic*, as in *comic(al), historic(al)* and *geographic(al). Liturgy* does not make an adjective "liturgic" but *liturgical. Theatre* makes *theatrical*. The noun *pharmacy* obviously caused difficulty in the formation of a connected adjective, and eventually the peculiar *pharmaceutical* appeared.

Although a grammatical rather than a spelling matter, a subject for interesting debate is the treatment of those nouns ending in the plural form *ics*. Should we say "Mathematics *are* his strong point" or "Mathematics *is* . . ."? Should we say "Politics *was* the main topic of his conversation" or "Politics *were* . . ."? There is no fixed rule. Logically, *a* subject or *an* academic sphere of learning is regarded as singular, and takes the singular verb form. My Canadian and American friends wonder why we abbreviate "mathematics" to the plural "maths" when they call the subject "math". The wonderment is mutual.

Interpolation: -ous and -ic

Although laymen may be hazy about the suffixes *-ous* and *-ic*, in chemistry scientists have been very cunning in seizing both to indicate definite differences in certain matters. For instance, most people know about *sulphuric* acid, and some may have heard about *sulphurous* acid and thought it was the same thing. There is a distinct chemical difference, however, just as there are differences between *ferric* and *ferrous* iron compounds, *cupric* and *cuprous* copper compounds, *nitric* and *nitrous* nitrogen compounds, and *phosphoric* and *phosphorous* phosphorus compounds. For the benefit of those readers who may follow newspapers in the matter of spelling, I emphasise that the element is *phosphorus*, not *phosphorous*.

Besides the adjective *metalliferous* mentioned earlier, there is another adjective, *metallic*, and in both the *l* is doubled. In some applications there is little or no difference; thus, a metalliferous mineral is the same as a metallic mineral, but if the noun "substance" is used rather than "mineral" the adjective is normally *metallic*. A mine producing ores is a metalliferous mine, not a metallic mine. It is customary to speak of a metallic sound, a metallic taste, or a metallic thread, when the other adjective would be unsuitable.

-ary

I have pointed out (page 56) how from the nouns *devolution*, *evolution* and *revolution* we can obtain the adjectives *devolutionary*, *evolutionary* and *revolutionary*. In these examples the suffix *-ary* is directly attached to the noun to form the adjective, and, indeed, this is the usual practice, other examples being *budget(ary)*, *diet(ary)*, *element(ary)*, *inflation(ary)* and *unit(ary)*. In *exemplary* there is a slight modification of the noun *example*, and in *voluntary* there is modification of *volunteer*.

Some other *-ary* adjectives are not *directly* formed from nouns—for example, *contrary*, *culinary*, *literary*, *military*, *necessary*, *pulmonary* and *sumptuary*. The suffix also finds its way into nouns, by association or along etymological routes, examples being *antiquary*, *apothecary* and *luminary*.

-ar

The suffix *-ar* is part of some nouns but is also attached to a number of nouns to make adjectives. Some conversions are regular, the suffix being simply added to the noun, as in *column(ar)* and *line(ar)*, without any amendment. Other nouns ending in *e*, however, unlike *line*, lose the *e* to give, for example: *molecule, molecular*; *nodule, nodular*; *vehicle, vehicular*. Some nouns ending in *e* not only lose it but adopt a *u*, making *angular* from *angle* and *titular* from *title*. In the case of some nouns ending in *us* these two letters are replaced by *ar*, as in: *annulus, annular*; *nucleus, nuclear*.

Peninsula makes *peninsular*, an adjective which unfortunately many people, and some newspapers, use as the noun. The noun *spatula* makes *spatular*, but another version of the adjective with the same meaning is *spatulate*. The adjective *regular* is not formed from a noun and a suffix but is derived from a Latin root meaning "rule". *Lunar* is derived etymologically from *moon*, and an adjective not found in older dictionaries is *sonar*, which is derived etymologically from *sound*.

-ful

There are many adjectives ending in *-ful* derived from nouns, the straightforward practice being to add the suffix to the basic word. There was a time when the suffix was given a double *l* as in the word *full* itself, but convenience—perhaps printers' convenience—led to its elimination. Examples are not hard to find. Here is a short list: *art(ful)*; *boast(ful)*; *care(ful)*; *doubt(ful)*; *event(ful)*; *fear(ful)*; *joy(ful)*; *master(ful)*; *sin(ful)*; *taste(ful)*; *wonder(ful)*.

Awful originally meant "inspiring awe" (with the *e* dropped), but because of its modern colloquial sense the word is now sometimes spelt "aweful" when the original meaning is required. *Dreadful* originally meant "inspiring dread" rather than, as now, "disagreeable" or "horrid".

In the case of some nouns ending in *y* the *y* is replaced by *i* before the suffix, to give: *beauty, beautiful*; *bounty, bountiful*;

fancy, fanciful. In each of these, of course, the adjective means "full of . . .". Where the noun refers to a container, to form another noun, however, the *y* is retained, as in *lorryful.*

Wilful is the accepted form of "will(ful)" with an *l* eliminated. *Hateful* should mean "full of hate", but its application has been transferred to the thing hated. *Grateful,* from the noun *gratitude,* is simpler than "gratitudeful". It, too, is sometimes transferred; a person refers to his "grateful thanks" when it is *he* who is grateful. The misapplication of *pitiful* is discussed on page 129.

Meaningful should be as respectable as *meaningless,* but the word has got into the wrong hands and is used indiscriminately by people who indulge in meaningless verbiage.

The suffix *-ful* can be applied also to nouns to make other nouns, as we shall see later.

-less

The common suffix *-less,* attached to nouns to make adjectives, gives the opposite meaning to the suffix *-ful.* Not that every *-ful* adjective can readily take *-less.* Consider the first list in the previous section.

Artless, careless, doubtless, fearless, sinless and *tasteless* are all acceptable. But there are no commonly recognisable words "boastless", "masterless" and "wonderless". Nor can we recognise the existence of "awless", "dreadless", "beautiless", "bountiless", "willess" and "hateless". The opposite of *grateful* is not "grateless" but *ungrateful. Meaningless,* as explained, is itself full of meaning.

-al, -ial, -eal

The suffix *-al* is not only an extension of *-ic* to form *-ical* in the manner explained on page 64, to give words such as *comical* and *historical.* It can also be independent of *-ic* and be a suffix in itself.

Unless the basic noun ends in *e* the suffix is usually a simple addition, as in *autumn(al), exception(al), function(al), hexagon(al), incident(al), sensation(al)* and *verb(al).* Interesting exceptions include: *abdomen, abdominal; benefit, beneficial; contract, contractual; crux, crucial; foetus, foetal; glottis, glottal.* In *glottis* there is a double *t* already, and although the verbs *acquit* and *rebut* (page 42) end in a single *t* this is doubled to form the nouns *acquittal* and *rebuttal*. The noun *digit* also ends in a single *t*, but in the conversion to the adjective *digital* the *t* remains single.

Where the basic noun ends in *e* the *e* is usually dropped to give, for example, the following: *adjective, adjectival*; *agriculture, agricultural*; *anticline, anticlinical*; *centre, central*; *doctrine, doctrinal*; *spectre, spectral*. *Line* is an exception; besides making an adjective *linear* (already discussed) it makes another, *lineal*, which pertains to a line of family descent.

Some nouns ending in *ce* behave as in the following examples, with the *e* dropped: *face, facial*; *finance, financial*; *province, provincial*; *race, racial*; *sacrifice, sacrificial*; *truce, trucial*.

Yet other nouns ending in *ce* are given adjectival endings in *tial*, as in the following examples (again with the *e* dropped): *consequence, consequential*; *deference, deferential*; *essence, essential*; *influence, influential*; *palace, palatial*; *providence, providential*; *space, spatial*; *substance, substantial*.

As a direct suffix, *-ial* is found in *tangent(ial)* and *torrent(ial)*; yet the similar *monument* forms *monumental*. The direct *-eal* suffix is found in *ether(eal)*.

The construction of *spatial* from *space* is curious when the adjectives from *face* and *race* are *facial* and *racial*. As noted earlier, another adjective from *space* is *spacious*. *Spatial* pertains to the subject of space in general; *spacious* implies that there is plenty of room.

In the case of some nouns ending in *y* the *y* is dropped and replaced by *ial*, as in: *actuary, actuarial*; *artery, arterial*; *industry, industrial*; *remedy, remedial*. (*Industry* forms another adjective *industrious*, which is different from *industrial*.) *Periphery* is an exception, making not "peripherial" but *peripheral*.

There are several adjectives ending in *-al*, *-ial* or *-eal* which are not directly formed from nouns but have strong etymological connections, examples being *arboreal, diurnal, dual, fiscal, floral, funereal, legal, maternal, prandial, radial, sidereal* and *terrestrial*.

-ate

Spatulate, mentioned earlier as an alternative to *spatular*, is one of the few adjectives ending in the suffix *-ate* which are directly derived from nouns. Another is *roseate* (coloured rose-pink) as in "The roseate hues of early dawn" (C. F. Alexander). There are, however, several *-ate* adjectives which are not directly connected with nouns, such as *cognate, desolate, duplicate* and *oblate*. *Pulmonate*, meaning "equipped with lungs", is different from *pulmonary*, which means "pertaining to the lungs".

-ine

A delta is one kind of river-mouth, an estuary is another. Yet the adjective from *delta* (page 63) is *deltaic*, and the adjective from *estuary* is *estuarine*. The suffix *-ine* is perhaps the most attractive of all, and gives rise to some lovely words; for example: *adamant, adamantine; alkali, alkaline; alp, alpine; coral, coralline; crystal, crystalline; Florence, Florentine; lake, lacustrine.* I admit that *asinine* from *ass* is not very attractive. *Sanguine* is now only remotely connected with blood, its usual modern meaning being "hopeful, optimistic", this state of mind having originally been attributed to the state of one's blood. *Sanguinary* ("bloody, bloodthirsty") is a different word altogether.

-ian, -ean, -ese

I have referred to the suffix *-ish* in its application to nationality and language. The suffix *-ian*, also, can be attached to proper nouns—names of people or places—to form adjectives of nationality, of geography, of language, of kind, or of some connection. Such adjectives include: of people: *Christ(ian), Churchill(ian), Georg(ian)* (*e* dropped); and of places: *Boston(ian), Eton(ian), Paris(ian), Mar(t)(ian)* (*s* of *Mars* replaced by *t*).

Where the *a* or *ia* is already part of the proper noun, *n* only is added, as in *Africa(n), Australia(n), Russia(n)*. This is especially the case with the English names of languages, such as *Persia(n)* and *Yugoslavia(n)*. In the development of English special treatment has been given to the English spelling of such adjectives as *Norwegian* (from *Norway*) and *Flemish* (from *Flanders*). Where the English equivalent of a name ends in *y* the adjective is formed by replacing the *y* by *ian*, as in *Italian* and *Hungarian*.

Inhabitants of some British cities have given themselves names which have no *direct* spelling connection with the city-names but which are usually understood, examples being

Dundonian (Dundee), *Glaswegian* (Glasgow), *Liverpudlian* (Liverpool), *Mancunian* (Manchester) and *Novocastrian* (Newcastle).

Greek, applied to nationality and language, is not the same as *Grecian*, which means "pertaining to Greece" or "having the characteristics of a Greek". For example, we speak of "a Grecian vase" and "a Grecian nose". The people of Etruria, incidentally, were not "Etrurians" but *Etruscans*.

The suffix *-ean* does similar work to *-ian*, but is largely restricted to adjectives connected with places and people. Where the basic proper noun ends in *es* this ending is replaced by *ean*, as in: *Antipodes, Antipodean; Archimedes, Archimedean; Hebrides, Hebridean*. Where the basic noun ends in *e, an* is added, as in *Europe(an)*. Where the basic noun ends in a consonant the suffix is a simple addendum, as in *Tyrol(ean)*. *Jacobean* is a derivative of *Jacobus*, or *James*.

The existence of two similar suffixes can be confusing, especially as some of the adjectives formed can be spelt either way. *Shakespeare*, for instance can form *Shakespearian* or *Shakesperean*. The master himself sometimes used the spelling "Shakespere".

Another suffix used in adjectives of nationality and language is *-ese*, as in *Chinese, Japanese, Portuguese*. It is also used in adjectives pertaining to styles of writing or of diction, as in *journalese*.

Apart from its use as a suffix in the formation of geographical and linguistic adjectives, *-ian* is used in the formation of many other words which can be either nouns or adjectives, such as *vegetarian* and *octogenarian*, but more often in the formation of nouns.

It is sometimes thought that because of its meaning, and the spelling, *riparian* is derived in a corrupt way from the noun *river*. It is true that the adjective means "associated with rivers", but the word is derived from a Latin root meaning the *bank* of the river, not the river itself; hence we have "riparian rights".

-en

The suffix *-en* attached to a few nouns conveys a meaning of "made of", "consisting of" or "of the nature of". Usually it is a simple addendum, as in *earth(en), flax(en), gold(en), hemp(en),* *wheat(en)* and *wood(en)*. In the case of *wool* the *l* is doubled to give *woollen*, and *brass* gives the irregular *brazen*. Archaic examples of the use of the suffix are *lead(en)*, *leather(n)* (no *e*), *oak(en)*, *oat(en)*, *silk(en)* and *wax(en)*, words which are so pleasant that it seems a pity that they are not seen more often.

-esque

There are a few adjectives converted from nouns by the unusual suffix *-esque*, which means "in the manner of" or "reminiscent of". The following examples are commonly seen or heard: *arab, arabesque*; *picture, picturesque*; *statue, statuesque*. *Arabesque*, when used as a noun, can refer to a fanciful type of decoration, to an elaborate musical composition, or to a ballet position. *Grotesque* was originally a *noun* applied to an extravagantly ornamental or distorted design, and its use as an adjective came later.

-able, -ible

These two suffixes, as we have seen, attach themselves to numerous verbs to form adjectives. They are attracted also to a great number of nouns, as in the following examples:
-able: action(able), fashion(able), honour(able), marriage(able).
-ible: access(ible), contempt(ible), forc(ible).

It should be noted that the *e* of *marriage* is retained but the *e* of *force* dropped. The adjective *contemptible* (as explained earlier) does not mean the same as *contemptuous*.

Some *-able* and *-ible* adjectives are connected only etymologically, not directly, with verbs and nouns, but in view of the number of adjectives with these endings I shall give a list later in the book.

-ose

The suffix *-ose* (denoting fullness, abundance, or possession of a quality) forms adjectives from bases which can be nouns (occasionally), other adjectives, or related Latin root-words. For example, *bellicose* (warlike) is from *bellum* (war); *comatose* is from the noun *coma*; *grandiose* is from the adjective *grand*; *jocose* is from *jocus* (joke); *morose* is from *morosus* (sullen, peevishly self-willed); *verbose* is from *verbum* (word). Except for *comatose*, these adjectives can form nouns: *bellicosity, grandiosity, jocosity, moroseness, verbosity*.

The other application of *-ose* is in chemical words such as *cellulose, dextrose* and *glucose*.

-iac

The suffix *-iac* is found in adjectives derived from nouns and in nouns derived from other nouns. Adjectives from nouns include *demoniac* from *demon*, *elegiac* from *elegy*, and *iliac* (iliac artery) from *ilium*. Nouns formed from other nouns include *insomniac* from *insomnia*, *kleptomaniac* from *kleptomania*, and *maniac* from *mania*. *Cardiac*, which can be adjective or noun, has only an etymological connection with *heart*, and *maniac* leads to the adjective *maniacal*. In chemistry, *sal ammoniac* is a compound related to *ammonia*.

PARTICIPLES AS ADJECTIVES

The present participle of a verb is often used as an adjective. Usually it ends in *ing*, as in *charming* (lady, for instance), *doting* (parents), *frightening* (incident), *moving* (experience), *spelling* (problem), *travelling* (salesman). Almost any present participle can be used as an adjective in some connection.

Past participles also can lend themselves to adjectival use, but less commonly than present participles. Past participles ending in *ed*, for example, give *cancelled* (appointment), *enthralled* (audience), *lapsed* (subscription), *rejected* (suitor), *unparalleled* (magnificence). Past participles ending in *en* give such expressions as *bitten* (apple), *cloven* (hoof), *stricken* (deer), *stolen* (purse).

The use of participles as adjectives, briefly outlined here for the sake of completeness, is generally understood, and no more need be said.

CONVERSION OF NOUNS TO VERBS

We have seen how verbs can be converted to nouns by the addition of suffixes. Conversely, some nouns can be converted to related verbs by the addition of other suffixes, such as *-en* (or *-n*), *-ify* (or *-fy*), *-ise* (or *-ize*), and *-ate*. Not to be forgotten, however, are the prefixes *en-*, *em-* and *dis-*.

-en (or -n)

The suffix *-en* is more usually attached to adjectives than to nouns. It is true that the noun *length* produces *lengthen*, and *strength* produces *strengthen*, but it can be argued that the basic words are the adjectives *long* and *strong*. The verb *heighten* is legitimately regarded as being derived from the noun *height* rather than the adjective *high*. The constant use of this suffix does not warrant any more discussion, but the obvious rule may be mentioned that, if the basic noun ends in *e*, *n* only is added as in *haste(n)*.

-ify (or -fy)

In the use of *-ify* modification of the basic noun is sometimes necessary, as in: *beauty, beautify*; *example, exemplify*; *fruit, fructify*; *glory, glorify*; *stupor, stupefy*. No modification is needed in cases like *person(ify)* and *solid(ify)*. Notes on the verbs derived from *liquid* will be found below.

Some *-ify* verbs, though not directly derived from English nouns, have strong etymological connections, such as *deify, magnify, petrify* and *sanctify*.

The noun *modification*, which I have used often, is derived from the verb *modify* ("to alter, but only moderately"), and this in turn is derived from the noun *mode* ("manner, way of doing"), the final *e* being dropped.

-ise (or- ize)

Examples of the use of the suffix as a direct appendage are: *carbon(ise)*, *idol(ise)*, *liquid(ise)*. In *glamour* and *vapour* the *u* is dropped to give *glamorise* and *vaporise*.

The question of choice between *-ise* and *-ize* does not exist in *all* cases, and is discussed at greater length on page 85.

I am reluctant to include, as examples, *synthesis, synthesise,* and *analysis, analyse,* as it is probable that the verbs appeared before the nouns.

-ate

Most verbs ending in *ate* are not *directly* derived from nouns, but there are a few which are. Such direct conversions, in which the suffix is added to the basic noun, include: *carbon(ate)*, *hyphen(ate)*, *liquid(ate)*. (*Carbon* forms two verbs, *carbonate* and *carbonise*, but *carbonate* is usually a noun.)

Conversions involving slight modification of the basic noun include: *action, activate*; *motion, motivate*; *vaccine, vaccinate*. *Acid* forms *acidulate*. An interesting example of unexpected construction is *filtrate*, which is *not* a verb. The verb is *filter*, and the filtrate is the liquid which passes through the filtering medium.

It is curious that although the verb *consolidate* is understood to mean "make solid" (*solid* being a noun or an adjective), there is neither a noun "consolid" nor a verb "solidate". The verb *decorate* is not derived from, but is etymologically related to, the French noun *décor*, the adoption of which in English is of fairly recent origin. Many *-ate* verbs, in fact, have only etymological connections with their basic nouns, such as *adumbrate, exculpate, legislate* and *terminate*. *Fenestrate* ("make a window") is derived from the French noun *fenêtre*.

A great many verbs ending in *ate* are not derived from nouns at all, and therefore have no place in our present discussion.

Interpolation: liquid

From the noun *liquid* are derived three different verbs with different meanings, each of which forms a secondary noun: *liquefy, liquefaction*; *liquidise, liquidisation*; *liquidate, liquidation*. Brief (not necessarily complete) definitions of the three verbs are as follows:

liquefy: convert solid to liquid, melt;

liquidise: convert solid to liquid by physical means, as in a mixer or pulveriser;

liquidate: bring to an end, pay off, wind up.

Liquid is also used as an adjective, and, in a linguistic sense, is found in such expressions as "liquid *l*". (See carillon, page 114).

Prefixes en-, em-

Many nouns can be converted to verbs by the prefix *en-*, which

is always a simple addition. Examples, not hard to find, are *en(case)*, *en(courage)*, *en(danger)*, *en(joy)*, *en(snare)* and *en(trust)*.

Allied to *en-* is the prefix *em-*, which, attracted to appropriate nouns, forms (for example) the verbs *em(balm)*, *em(bank)*, *em(body)*, *em(brace)* and *em(power)*.

Prefix dis-

Dis-, an exceedingly versatile prefix, can be attached to nouns to form verbs, to verbs to form other verbs, and to adjectives to form other adjectives. Essentially it is a negative-forming prefix, usually conveying a meaning of "opposite" or "away from", and as examples of its attachment to nouns to form verbs the following should suffice for illustration: *dis(band)*, *dis(bar)*, *dis(courage)* (opposite of *encourage*), *dis(cover)*, *dis(grace)*, *dis(honour)* and *dis(illusion)*. Other examples are given on page 94.

Cases where the noun and the verb are the same word

There are numerous cases where a noun can be used as a verb, examples being *attack, cook, honour, manufacture, noise* ("noise it abroad"), *paper* ("paper the room"), *polish, service* and *sound. Summons* is a singular noun with a legal connotation giving a similar verb meaning "to issue a summons". The verb *summon* has a different meaning.

CONVERSION OF NOUNS TO OTHER NOUNS

Several suffixes are used to convert nouns to other words which are still nouns but mean something different. The following will be considered: *-age, -ful, -ry* and *-y, -cy, -hood, -ship, -ate, -ure, -ic, -ster, -dom, -ism, -ee* and *-eer*.

-age

Sometimes the suffix is a direct addition, as in *acre(age)*, *broker(age)* and *front(age)*. In *usage* the *e* of the basic noun *use* has been dropped. (*Use* can also be a verb.) *Assembly* can be converted to *assemblage*, which admittedly means much the same.

-ful

A *full spoon* (adjective and noun) contains a *spoonful* (noun).

There are many such words, all ending in one *l*. If there is a problem, it lies in deciding on the plural form. Is it *spoonsful* or *spoonfuls*? As the derived noun is a measure of quantity it should be *spoonfuls*, just as we speak of pints, tons and miles, or, to fall in with metric custom, of litres, tonnes and kilometres. Other *-ful* nouns derived from other nouns include *cupful, handful, houseful* and *mouthful*. The construction of *-ful* adjectives from verbs and nouns has been considered (pages 53 and 66).

-ry, -y

Examples of the use of either of these similar suffixes spring readily to the mind. Usually the suffix is a simple addition to the basic noun, even when this ends in *e*, as *bigot(ry), burglar(y), citizen(ry), knave(ry), machine(ry), pageant(ry), rock(ery), rook(ery), scene(ry)* and *weapon(ry)*. Exceptions include: *grain, granary; statue, statuary*.

-cy

This suffix is seldom applied to the basic noun, some modification usually being necessary. Examples are: *lunatic, lunacy; magistrate, magistracy; president, presidency; pirate, piracy; primate, primacy; resident, residence, residency* (three nouns); *tenant, tenancy; truant, truancy*. No modification is needed in the following examples, where the suffix is a straightforward addendum: *bankrupt(cy), captain(cy), chaplain(cy), colonel(cy), viscount(cy)*.

-hood

The suffix *-hood* has a limited application to collective humanity, and is added directly to the basic noun to form, for example, *boy(hood), child(hood), girl(hood), man(hood), priest(hood)* and *woman(hood)*. We saw earlier that attached to an adjective it can form *falsehood*.

-ship

Another suffix applied to nouns of humanity to form other nouns, usually to indicate a state or an office, is *-ship*, which is added to the basic noun directly, as in *friend(ship), head(ship), judge(ship), owner(ship), scholar(ship)* and *trustee(ship)*.

-ate

An *emir* rules over an Arab *emirate*. The Roman *triumvirate* was composed of three *triumvirs*. An *opiate* was originally a drug prepared from *opium*, and the word is now applied to substances which have similar effects but not necessarily similar origins. A body of *electors* is an *electorate*. These are all examples of the use of the suffix in the conversion of basic nouns to other nouns, and although it has other uses (for example, in the conversion of nouns to verbs described on page 74), they do not concern us in this section. It should perhaps be mentioned, however, that the suffix is a useful indicative part of the names of some chemical compounds; for instance, the *sulphate* of an element is different from the sulphide and the *chlorate* from the chloride.

-ure

Unless the basic noun ends in *e*, the suffix is a direct addition, as in *forfeit(ure)* and *portrait(ure)*. (I have already referred to the use of *forfeit* as a verb.) The *e* of *candidate* is dropped to give *candidature*. A papal ambassador at a foreign court is a *nuncio*, and he is a member of the *nunciature*. *Imposture* is the act of an *impostor*. *Nomenclature*, although not derived directly from an English noun, is based on the Latin word *nomen* (*name*).

The addition of the suffix to verbs to form nouns is discussed on page 43.

-ic

The suffix *-ic* forms adjectives more readily than it forms nouns, as I have explained at some length. Although there are several nouns ending in *-ic*, few of them are derived directly from other nouns. One is *philippic*, and even here the basic word is a proper noun, *Philip*. The word was originally applied to orations of Demosthenes against Philip of Macedon, but now is applied to any acrimonious declamation.

Another proper noun is *Muse*, one of the nine from mythology, from which the noun *music* is derived. Rather obscurely, the Muses were also responsible for the noun *mosaic*, a design composed of small stones. Etymological connections are found in *logic* (a noun-noun connection from a Greek word meaning "speech or reason") and *rubric* (an adjective-noun from a Latin word meaning "red"). Rubrics are the instructions printed in red in some editions of the *Book of Common Prayer*, and this ecclesiastical connection prompts me to refer to the noun-noun conversion *bishopric*, a word for a bishop's office or diocese.

-ster

On page 59, writing about the word *youngster*, derived from the adjective *young*, I said that the suffix *-ster* was usually applied to nouns to form other nouns. As a direct addition it forms words like *prankster, punster, rhymester, songster* and *trickster*. Sometimes such nouns are used facetiously, but the suffix has a few worthier applications. A maker of malt, for example, could be a "malter", but somehow *maltster* sounds far more interesting. I have already dealt with the attachment of the suffix to the verb *spin* to form the hard-working *spinster*.

-dom

Nouns ending with the suffix *-dom* are formed from basic nouns to denote power, jurisdiction, office or condition. There is no need for any alteration of the basic word in conversion to (for example) *duke(dom), earl(dom), king(dom)* or *official(dom)*. *Wisdom*, as noted elsewhere in this book, is derived from the adjective *wise*. "By my *halidom*" was an old oath now often quoted in historical novels, *hali* being Old English for *holy*.

-ism

The addition of the suffix *-ism* to adjectives to form nouns has been discussed (page 57), but there are cases in which it can be attached to nouns. Examples are *cannibal(ism), journal(ism), pauper(ism)* and *Quaker(ism)*. *Criticism* should perhaps be regarded as derived from the verb *criticise* rather than the noun *critic*. The noun *dogmatism* is related to the noun *dogma*, but *pragmatism* (as already pointed out) can be derived only from the adjective *pragmatic* as there is no English noun "pragma".

-ee

The French origin of the suffix *-ee* in its relation to verbs was explained on page 46. The suffix also is applied in the conversion of nouns to other nouns *usually* to denote a recipient, examples being *grantee* from *grant* (used as a noun) and *legatee* from *legacy*. There is one case, however, where the suffix does *not* denote the recipient. On page 46 I used *mortgage* as a verb in the sense of mortgaging one's property, but it could equally be a noun, as the borrower (*mortgagor* or *mortgager*), by means of a *mortgage* (noun), borrows money from the *mortgagee*.

The suffix is used also to indicate some connection between the formed noun and the basic noun; thus, a *bargee* is concerned with a *barge* and a *devotee* feels *devotion* towards his hobby or interest.

-eer

The suffix *-eer* denotes a person who is concerned with, or is responsible for, the thing forming the base of the word. Examples are *chariot(eer)*, *musket(eer)* and *pamphlet(eer)*.

CONVERSION OF ADJECTIVES TO VERBS

When an adjective is applied to a noun the sense of application may be conveyed by means of a verb which is formed by the addition of a suffix or a prefix to the adjective.

A common suffix for the purpose is *-en* (or *-n*), which gives such direct conversions as: *black(en)*, *bright(en)*, *deep(en)*, *loose(n)*, *sweet(en)*, *tight(en)*, *white(n)*. Modification of the basic word is found in: *high. heighten*; *long, lengthen*; *strong, strengthen*. (These examples were discussed on page 73, "Conversion of Nouns to Verbs".)

With *fat* the *t* is doubled to make *fatten*, the archaic *fatted* (calf) being retained in the parable of the Prodigal Son. In adjectives ending in *d* the *d* is doubled, as in *gladden*, *madden*, *redden* and *sadden*.

Some adjectives, inexplicably, can be used as verbs without the addition of *-en*, examples being *blind, cool, dry, foul, free, lame* and *thin*. The refusal of some adjectives to accept the suffix is also inexplicable: thus we say *moisten* but not "wetten", *quicken* but not "slowen", *thicken* but not "thinnen", *sharpen* but not "blunten". The adjective *hot* gives the verb (and the noun) *heat*. The expression "hotted up" is an unpleasant colloquialism the use of which is not to be encouraged.

The suffix *-ify* is more commonly attached to nouns, as we

have seen, but in a few cases it can be attached to adjectives to form verbs, as in *falsify* from *false* and *uglify* from *ugly*. There is modification of the adjective in the conversion of *clear* to *clarify*. In the verb *rectify* the base is from a Latin word meaning "right".

Some adjectives are converted to verbs with the aid of prefixes. For example, the prefix *en-* produces *en(dear)*, *en(feeble)*, *en(large)*, *en(noble)* and *en(rich)*. *Encumber*, as mentioned elsewhere, is the verb from the adjective *cumbrous*. Rarer prefixes give us: *dense, condense*; *strange, estrange*; *new, renew*; *fine, refine*.

ADVERBS

Most literate people know what an adverb is and what it does. As an adjective qualifies a noun an adverb qualifies a verb to describe the manner or circumstances in which the action is done, and the commonest way of forming an adverb is to add the suffix *-ly* to the appropriate adjective. Thus we get *curious(ly)*, *economical(ly)*, *faithful(ly)*, *occasional(ly)*, *pleasant(ly)*, *strong(ly)* and *slow(ly)*. An adverb can also be used to describe an adjective, as in *tremendously happy*.

When the adjective ends in *y*, this is replaced by *i* before the *ly*, examples being: *gay, gaily*; *happy, happily*; *merry, merrily*. Confusion is sometimes caused when the adjective itself ends in *ly*, but the same rule applies, with such results as: *friendly, friendlily*; *jolly, jollily*; *lovely, lovelily*; *naughty, naughtily*; *wily, wilily*; *ugly, uglily*. It is true that some adjectives of this type do not readily lend themselves to adverbial construction. In such cases, for example, "He behaved in a cowardly way" is preferable to "He behaved cowardlily".

From the adjective *kind* an unusual extension *kindly* has been formed, which besides being an adverb is also an adjective and itself produces another adverb, *kindlily*. *Sickly* is a similar extension of *sick*, but I have never seen an adverb "sicklily". A peculiar adjective is *likely* ("a likely story"), which very occasionally you may find as the base for an adverb *likelily*.

Adjectives ending in *e* do not all receive the same treatment. In most cases the *e* is retained and the suffix added normally, as in: *active(ly)*, *brave(ly)*, *sincere(ly)*, *strange(ly)*. The *e* is dropped from adjectives ending in *le* after a consonant, to give the following: *ample, amply*; *forcible, forcibly*; *humble, humbly*; *simple, simply*; *single, singly*; *subtle, subtly*; *terrible, terribly*; *treacle, treacly*. When *le* comes after a vowel the *e* is usually retained, as in *docile(ly)*, *hale(ly)*, *sole(ly)* and *vile(ly)*. *Whole*, however, as an exception, makes not "wholely" but *wholly*.

Three words which are both adjective and adverb are *fast*, *hard* and *tight*. "Run fast", "Work hard" and "Hold tight" are legitimate commands, but I should say "Screw it tightly". There is no adverb "fastly" but there is a word *hardly*, the adverbial use of which should be confined to the meaning of *scarcely*, so that "hardly any money" is the same as "scarcely any money". Occasionally "hardly earned" may be seen, but, perhaps because the sense of this can be ambiguous, "hard-earned" with the linking hyphen is preferable. The obsolete expression "hard by" meant "near".

A peculiarity of English is that although there is an adverb *badly* there is no adverb *goodly*. The word for this, the direct opposite of *badly*, is *well*, as in "Do it well". *Goodly* is an archaic adjective which had various vague meanings connected with *good* ("a goodly sum", for example), but it is not an adverb.

There is a fairly common practice of adding *ly* to past-tense or past-participle formations to produce adverbs like *admitted(ly)*, *alleged(ly)*, *hurried(ly)*, *supposed(ly)* and *undoubted(ly)*. Care should be taken, however, to avoid the practice if the result sounds unwieldy or unnatural. Some present participles also can take *ly* to form adverbs, as in *joking(ly)*, *laughing(ly)*, *loving(ly)* and *menacing(ly)*.

I should point out that the adjectives *quick* and *slow* are very often misused as adverbs, either through ignorance or lack of space. "Get rich quick" is as bad as the official warning seen on roads, "Go slow". As for "new laid eggs"—well, perhaps only a fussy pedant would insist on "newly-laid eggs".

PART III

Spelling Rules and Conventions

Having dealt at some length with the formation of words, and discussed points of spelling as they arose, I shall now examine some spelling matters in detail. I tried to devise a logical sequence in the following dissertation but decided that as there is much in the subject of spelling that is illogical any such attempt would be futile. The fact that one section of this chapter precedes another, therefore, does not necessarily mean that it is the more important.

-ISE OR -IZE?

Etymologists have tended to add to the confusion that exists in the vexed question of choice, if any, between these two suffixes. Some have asserted that as most traditional English verbs are ultimately of Greek composition, in which the root contains the equivalent of *izo*, the *ize* spelling should be used for most verbs, *ise* being adopted for those verbs which are not of Greek origin. If this were to be a "rule" to be remembered it would be useless to most people, who have to write countless things every day.

The French changed the *z* into *s* long ago, and those French infinitives (mainly derived from Greek through Latin) which correspond with our own always end in *iser*. While nearly all *ize* words may be spelt *ise* the converse does not hold. In British English some words are now never spelt with *z*, such as *advertise, advise, chastise, comprise, compromise, devise* and *exercise*. I emphasise (this is always *s*) "now" because in the eighteenth century many writers favoured *surprize* and *enterprize*.

If you use *ise* in nearly all cases you will be safe. *Recognise* can take *s*, though *recognize* is more common. The verb makes the noun *recognition*, or, much less commonly, *recognizance* (always with *z*) and *cognizance*. There is a slight difference in meaning between *cognition* (the act or faculty of perceiving) and *cognizance* (knowledge, notice, awareness).

It is interesting to observe that although the verb *criticise* can be spelt with either *s* or *z*, the noun *criticism* has no alternative, all *ism* nouns being spelt with *s*. In words in which there is a British choice between *s* and *z*, Americans normally use *z*. In words in which there is no choice, and are always spelt with *s*, America follows British practice. Although *analyse, catalyse, paralyse* and *synthesise* are spelt with *z* by Americans, our friends agree with our noun-spellings *analysis, catalysis, paralysis* and *synthesis*.

EI AND IE

There are numerous words in which the letters *e* and *i* occur together, either as *ei* or *ie*. In some words the combination produces the sound *ee*, and it is these which are our immediate concern. The hundreds of others in which the two letters occur together but which are not pronounced with a definite *ee* sound have no part in our present discussion.

One of the most commonly-remembered spelling rules in English, which we were taught in our first schooling, is: "*i* before *e* except after *c*". This rule, I repeat, applies only to the words in which the combination produces the sound *ee*, as in *belief, chief, field, frieze, grief, niece, relief, retrieve, thief* and *tier*.

In none of these words is there a *c* before the *i*. Other words, in which the vowel sound is *preceded* by *c*, include *ceiling, conceive, deceive, perceive* and *receive*, in all of which *e* comes before *i*. The exceptions—all words with an *ee* sound—are so few that they can be easily remembered, and include *counterfeit, seize, weir* and *weird*. *Either* and *neither* can be pronounced as *ee* or *eye*, but if you prefer an *ee* sound these words, too, can be numbered with the exceptions.

L OR LL?

Words ending in *l* or *ll* sometimes give rise to doubts when they have to be converted to other words or parts of speech. Rather than try to describe the rules and customs governing the spelling of such words, I have simplified the matter by listing the various possible changes for selected words. This section is an extension of the notes on page 26.

Basic verb	Past tense and past participle	Present participle	Related noun (if any)
ail	ailed	ailing	ailment
anneal	annealed	annealing	annealment
annul	annulled	annulling	annulment
appal	appalled	appalling	
apparel	apparelled	apparelling	apparel
appeal	appealed	appealing	appellant, appeal
befall	befell	befalling	
carol	carolled	carolling	carol
conceal	concealed	concealing	concealment
control	controlled	controlling	control, controller
distil	distilled	distilling	distillation, distiller
enthrall (enthral)	enthralled	enthralling	enthralment
equal	equalled	equalling	equality
excel	excelled	excelling	excellence
fall	fell, fallen	falling	fall
fell	felled	felling	feller (*of trees*)
fill	filled	filling	filler
fulfil	fulfilled	fulfilling	fulfilment
initial	initialled	initialling	initial
install	installed	installing	installation
instil	instilled	instilling	instillation
parallel	paralleled	paralleling	parallel
propel	propelled	propelling	propellant, propeller
repeal	repealed	repealing	repeal
repel	repelled	repelling	repellent
reveal	revealed	revealing	revelation

Conversions of -*ll* adjectives to nouns include: *dull, dullness*; *full, fullness*; *ill, illness*; *small, smallness*. Although the adjectives *dull* and *full* make *dullness* and *fullness*, occasionally *dulness* and *fulness* are seen. *Dull* can also be a verb, making *dulled* and *dulling*. *Full*, too, can be a verb, in the sense of dressing cloth with fuller's earth.

The noun *instalment* has no connection with the verb *install*, instalments being periodic payments (by hire-purchase, for instance) or parts of a serial story.

The single *l* after the *e* in *paralleled* will be noted. As I pointed out earlier, however, this past tense (and past participle used as an adjective) is seldom or never heard without its negative qualification, as in "unparalleled magnificence". Another interesting fact is that although the verb *propel* makes the noun *propellant*, *repel* makes *repellent*.

As a suffix for converting nouns to adjectives, -*ful*, meaning "full of", has only one *l*, and in *skilful* and *wilful* one *l* is dropped from the basic words *skill* and *will*.

There is the group of words prefixed by *al*- which is an abbreviation of *all*, as in *almighty, almost, already, altogether* and *always*. The fact that all these are "correct" does not mean that you can write "alright", which is all wrong. If you can remember to use *all right* you are showing your awareness of the written word.

Wool in British English makes the adjectives *woollen* and *woolly*. In America the first adjective is *woolen* and the second can be *wooly* or *woolly*. The dropping of one *l* where we use a double *l* is common practice in American English, to give such spellings as *equaled, leveled* and *traveler*, and *jewellery* is *jewelry*. I shall have more to say later about American spelling.

-ECTION OR -EXION?

In certain nouns there is a choice between the endings -*ection* and -*exion*, some philologists defending -*exion* as being *sometimes* correct on etymological grounds. *Connection* is sometimes written *connexion*, yet "correxion" is never seen. *Inflexion* is the normal spelling, and *inflection* is acceptable. *Reflexion* is seldom seen, but *complexion* is standard. *Bisection, dissection* and *section* are never spelt with *x*.

PLURALS

Most English nouns form plurals ending in *s* or *es*. There are, however, several other ways of indicating plurality, and representative lists of nouns and applicable plural endings are given below.

Singular	Plural	Singular	Plural
-um	*-a*	*-a*	*-ae*
addendum	addenda	alga	algae
agendum	agenda	antenna	antennae
bacterium	bacteria	formula	formulae
corrigendum	corrigenda	lacuna	lacunae
datum	data	larva	larvae
dictum	dicta	nebula	nebulae
erratum	errata		
gymnasium	gymnasia	*-is*	*-es*
medium	media	analysis	analyses
memorandum	memoranda	antithesis	antitheses
maximum	maxima	basis	bases
minimum	minima	crisis	crises
spectrum	spectra	emphasis	emphases
stratum	strata	metamorphosis	metamorphoses
		neurosis	neuroses
-on	*-a*	synthesis	syntheses
criterion	criteria	thesis	theses
octahedron	octahedra		
phenomenon	phenomena	*-us*	*-era*
		corpus	corpera
-us	*-i*	genus	genera
bacillus	bacilli	opus	opera
cactus	cacti		
focus	foci	*-a*	*-ata*
fungus	fungi	dogma	dogmata
gladiolus	gladioli	stigma	stigmata
locus	loci		
narcissus	narcissi	*-en*	
nucleus	nuclei	brother	brethren
radius	radii	child	children
tumulus	tumuli	man	men
		ox	oxen
		woman	women

Although the archaic *brethren* has been included in the list for illustration, the usual plural, of course, is *brothers*. Not included in the list are two -*im* plurals, *cherub(im)* and *seraph(im)*.

In the case of nouns ending in *y* after a consonant the *y* is replaced by *ies*, as in *beauties*, *cities*, *cries*, *ladies* and *skies*. After a vowel the *y* is retained and *s* added, as in *boys*, *keys*, *quays*, *trays* and *monkeys*.

Plurals of nouns ending in *o* vary in their treatment. *Cargoes*, *echoes*, *grottoes*, *heroes*, *potatoes*, *tomatoes*, *tornadoes*, *vetoes* and *volcanoes* all take *e* between *o* and *s*. Plurals omitting the *e* include *avocados*, *autos*, *dynamos*, *folios*, *radios*, and *ratios*.

Nouns of Italian origin are sometimes given their native plural form, as in *graffiti* (from *graffito*), *libretti* (from *libretto*) and *soli* (from *solo*), but the plural of *solo* is often expressed as *soloes*. *Imbroglio* also is of Italian origin, but its English plural is usually *imbroglios*. French is well enough known in Britain to justify *bureaux* and *tableaux*.

Nouns ending in *f* (or *fe*) are inconsistent. Some take an ending *fs*, others *ves*, and others can take either, as shown in the following table.

Singular	Plural -fs	Singular	Plural -ves	Singular	Plural optional
chef	chefs	calf	calves	dwarf	dwarfs
chief	chiefs	elf	elves		dwarves
cliff	cliffs	half	halves	handker-	handker-
cuff	cuffs	hoof	hooves	chief	chiefs
gaff	gaffs	knife	knives		handker-
gaffe	gaffes	leaf	leaves		chieves
giraffe	giraffes	loaf	loaves	scarf	scarfs
proof	proofs	self	selves		scarves
puff	puffs	sheaf	sheaves	staff	staffs
roof	roofs	shelf	shelves		staves
serf	serfs	thief	thieves	wharf	wharfs
tiff	tiffs	wife	wives		wharves

Despite the plurals of *gladiolus* and *narcissus*—*gladioli* and *narcissi*—the plural of *crocus* is *crocuses*. Other -*us* nouns which take the -*es* plural are *circuses*, *lotuses*, *prospectuses*, *hiatuses*, *ignoramuses* and *octopuses*. For *hippotamus*, both *hippopotami* and *hippopotamuses* are acceptable, and for *rhinoceros* the plural is either the same singular word or *rhinoceroses*. *Iris* makes *irises*.

Nouns ending in *ch, sh, ss* or *x* take *es*, as in *churches, flushes, crosses* and *foxes*. (I have already referred to the exceptional *oxen*.) Nouns ending in *ix* or *ex* vary in treatment, giving, for example: *annex(e), annexes; apex, apexes* or *apices; appendix, appendices; index, indexes* or *indices; matrix, matrices*. (*Annex* can be spelt with or without the final *e*.)

I have given three examples of nouns ending in *on* which take the plural *a* (*criteria, octahedra* and *phenomena*). Many other nouns ending in *on*, however, take *s*, as in *aeons, chameleons, lexicons, neutrons, polygons, pantechnicons* and *rhododendrons*.

Most nouns ending in *s* take *es* for the plural, even *lens* (*lenses*) and *summons* (*summonses*), which seem to puzzle many. In some cases the singular and the plural are the same word, examples being *corps, innings, mews, series* and *species*. Some nouns are naturally plural and cannot be given singular forms, such as *pincers, pliers, pyjamas, scissors, shears* and *trousers*.

Finally, there are those irregular and inconsistent plurals which infuriate many people but add to the rich diversity of English: *booth, booths*, but *tooth, teeth; house, houses*, but *louse, lice*, and *mouse, mice; noose, nooses*, but *goose, geese*, and *mongoose, mongooses; boot, boots*, but *foot, feet*.

Surnames ending in *s* can perplex people when plurals are required, but needlessly so. They should be treated as most other normal nouns ending in *s* and given *es*, so that "the Jones" is wrong and "the Joneses" is right, as also are "the Mosses" and "the Blisses". Where possessives are concerned journalists often get themselves into a muddle, but I shall say more about this when I deal with the apostrophe.

I must conclude this section on plurals by deploring common mistakes by people who claim to be literate. One of the most serious, which is found regularly in the Press, on television and radio, is the treatment of plural nouns as singular, such as *criteria, data, media, phenomena* and *strata*.

FEMININE FORMS

Where a noun is definitely masculine it can usually be converted to the feminine form by addition of the suffix *-ess*, or *-ss*, as in *authoress*, *mayoress*, *priestess*, *princess* and *shepherdess*. The basic noun is modified in the following examples: *abbott, abbess*; *actor, actress*; *ambassador, ambassadress*; *duke, duchess*; *emperor, empress*; *governor, governess*; *hunter, huntress*; *marquis* (*marquess*), *marchioness*; *master, mistress*.

It should be mentioned that although a mayoress is the wife of a mayor, and thus always feminine, a mayor need not be a man. The chief citizen not uncommonly is a woman, who is the mayor or even the lord mayor. Similarly a chairman can be a woman ("Madam Chairman"), the title applying to the office and not to the individual. Use of the ridiculous modern term "chairperson", as far as I am concerned, is not to be encouraged.

A *clerkess* is known only in Scotland, or among Scots abroad.

Besides the *ess* (or *ss*) ending there are the irregular endings shown in the following examples: *administrator, administratrix*; *draughtsman, draughtswoman*; *executor, executrix*; *hero, heroine*; *rajah, ranee*; *testator, testatrix*; *tsar, tsarina*; *yachtsman, yachtswoman*.

Where there is no special feminine form of the noun, and it is *necessary* to signify the sex of the person concerned, it is usual to refer, for example, to a woman doctor, a woman painter, a woman teacher.

The femininity of some animals is denoted by *-ess*, as in *lioness* and *tigress*. Other females have special names, such as *bitch, mare* and *vixen*, but this is not the place for a comprehensive list.

COMPARATIVE FORMS OF ADJECTIVES

A few adjectives have their special forms of comparatives, easy examples being *bad, worse, worst*, and *good, better, best*. The second and third words of the groups mean "more bad" and "most bad" and "more good" and "most good".

Some adjectives make their comparatives by the direct addition of *er* and *est*, as in: *hard, harder, hardest*; *quiet, quieter, quietest*; *slow, slower, slowest*.

Where the basic adjective ends in *y* treatment is variable. After a consonant the *y* is usually dropped to give, for example:

dry, drier, dries; *gloomy, gloomier, gloomiest*; *happy, happier, happiest*; *ugly, uglier, ugliest*. *Gay,* where the *y* follows a vowel, makes *gayer* and *gayest*. *Shy* can follow two patterns, *shyer* and *shyest* and *shier* and *shiest*.

Where an adjective of one syllable ends in a single consonant after a "short" vowel the consonant is doubled to give, for example: *big, bigger, biggest*; *fat, fatter, fattest*; *hot, hotter, hottest*.

An example of a "long" vowel is provided by the adjective *far*, and here *th* is inserted for convenience of diction to make *farther* and *farthest*.

After other long vowels the final consonant stays single, as in: *clear, clearer, clearest*; *fair, fairer, fairest*; *poor, poorer, poorest*. When the long-vowel adjective ends in *e, r* or *st* is simply added, as in: *cute, cuter, cutest*; *large, larger, largest*; *rare, rarer, rarest*.

Many adjectives do not readily accept the *er* and *est* treatment, and for those it is necessary to use *more* and *most*. "The most beautiful woman" is obviously more pleasant to hear than "the beautifullest woman". Although I have written *more pleasant, pleasanter* would have been acceptable. *Some* adjectives, indeed, can take both *er-est* and *more-most* forms, the choice depending on euphony, rhythm and context.

Adjectives ending in *ous* refuse to accept *er* and *est*, and when Lewis Carroll makes Alice observe "curiouser and curiouser" the remark is confined to Wonderland.

COMPARATIVE FORMS OF ADVERBS

In theory there is nothing wrong with the sentence, "James runs quicklier than John", but in practice "James runs more quickly" is smoother. The *-lier* form is archaic but may have poetic or deliberately unusual applications. Adverbs ending in *ly* almost invariably need the *more* and *most* formations.

The *-er* and *-est* formations are restricted to those adverbs *not* ending in *ly*. We should therefore say, "He runs faster" (or "fastest"), "She works harder" (or "hardest").

The independent adverb *soon* easily makes *sooner* and *soonest*; but *often* and *seldom* take *more* and *most*.

Although earlier, on the subject of adverbs, I said that "Hold tight" was as legitimate as "Work hard" and "Run fast", I still prefer "Screw it more tightly" to "Screw it tighter". "Easier said than done" is an ungrammatical colloquialism, but trips off the tongue more smoothly than "More easily said . . ." or even "Easilier said . . .".

NEGATIVE FORMS OF WORDS

Prefixes making negatives are applicable to verbs, adjectives, nouns and adverbs. Examples of their use are listed below, and it will be seen that in most cases (modification being noted where necessary) the prefix is simply added to the base. (Appropriate negative prefixes for *-able* and *-ible* adjectives are given in the lists on page 96.)

Verbs with un-
unbend
undo
undress
unfasten
unhinge
unlatch
unmask
unquote
unroll
unseat

Verbs with dis-
disagree
disarm
disarrange
discourage
disenchant
disjoint
dismount
disown
displease
disqualify
dissuade

Verbs with mis-
misapply
misbehave
miscalculate
misconstrue
miscount
misjudge
mislead
mismanage
misplace
misquote
misspell
misunderstand

Verbs with de-
decipher
decompose
deconsecrate
decrease
defame
deform
degenerate
degrade
dehydrate

Adjectives with un-
unattached
unattractive
unhappy
unnatural
unpopular
unreasonable
unremitting
unrepentant
unsteady
unwanted

Adjectives with dis-
disadvantageous
disagreeable
discontinuous
disgraceful
dishonest
disillusioned
disloyal
disobedient
disorderly
displeased

Adjectives with im-
immaculate
immaterial
immature
immoderate
immodest
immoral
immovable
impermeable
impolite

Adjectives with mis-
miscast
misled
misused

Adjectives with il-
illegal
illegible
illegitimate
illiberal
illimitable
illiterate
illogical

Adjectives with in-
inaccessible
inactive
inaudible
incoherent
indecent
inefficient
inexperienced
inhuman
innocuous
insignificant

Adjective with ig-
ignoble

Adjectives with ir-
irredeemable
irreducible
irrefutable
irregular
irrelevant
irreligious
irremediable
irreparable
irresistible
irreverent
irrevocable

Adjectives with non-
non-commissioned
non-ferrous
non-playing
non-returnable
non-static
non-stick

Nouns with dis-
disadvantage
disaffection
disagreement
disarmament
disarray
disbelief
discomfort
discontent
discredit
disgrace

Nouns with mis-
misadventure
misalliance
misconception
misdeed
misdemeanour
misfire
misfortune
misrule
misuse

Nouns with de-
decomposition
defoliation
deformation
dehydration
demerit

Nouns with non-
non-acceptance
non-aggression
nonconformist
non-delivery
non-payment
nonsense
non-starter

Adverbs

In the main, the same prefixes are used for negative forms of adverbs as for negative adjectives. Where possible, the suffix -*ly* is a simple addendum, and where necessary slight changes are made to the basic forms. A final *e* is dropped, and a final *y* is replaced by *i*. Examples of negative adverbs (one for each prefix except *non*-) are: *unsteadily, disloyally, misguidedly, improbably, illegally, irrevocably, inaudibly, ignobly.*

Notes

In *discourage, dis-* replaces the *en-* of *encourage.* In *dissuade, dis-* replaces the *per-* of *persuade. Unquote* (verb) is "to close the quotation". *Misquote* is "to quote inaccurately".

Adjectives include adjectival participles. Adjectives with the prefix *de-* are excluded from the lists as they are derived from verbs which already carry the negative *de-* prefix, such as *deform(ed)* and *dehydrate(d).*

Most *non-* adjectives at present take the hyphen, exceptions being made in the case of established words like *nonsensical. Non-stick* is an adjective made from the verb *stick. Non-* nouns taking the hyphen are of comparatively recent origin, unlike established nouns like *nonconformist* and *nonsense.* Some of the *dis-* and *mis-* nouns are also verbs.

-ABLE AND -IBLE ADJECTIVES

As many adjectives ending in the suffixes -*able* and -*ible* can cause doubts as to which suffix to use, I give below a selection divided into fifty of each of the two categories. The appropriate negative prefixes also are shown.

-able		
in alienable	un creditable	in explicable
un alterable	in curable	in hospitable
in appreciable	un debatable	in imitable
un believable	in definable	un justifiable
in calculable	un demonstrable	un likeable
in capable	in dispensable	il limitable
in conceivable	un eatable	un manageable
in consolable	in estimable	im measurable
	in excusable	im movable

able—*cont.*

in numerable
un obtainable
im passable
un payable
im penetrable
im permeable
im practicable
im probable
un questionable
ir reconcilable
ir redeemable
ir refutable
ir remediable
ir reparable
ir revocable
in separable
un serviceable
in sufferable
in supportable
un touchable
un usable
un viable
in vulnerable
un wearable

-ible

in accessible
in admissible
in audible
in combustible
in compatible
in comprehensible
in compressible
in controvertible
in convertible
in corrigible
in corruptible
in credible
in defensible
in delible
in destructible
in digestible
in discernible
in distensible
in divertible
in divisible
in edible
in eligible
in exhaustible
in expensible

in expressible
in extensible
in fallible
in flexible
in frangible
in fusible
in gullible
un impressible
un intelligible
il legible
im miscible
in omissible
im passible
im perceptible
im permissible
im plausible
ir reducible
ir remissible
ir repressible
ir responsible
ir resistible
ir reversible
in sensible
in susceptible
in tangible
in visible

Notes

Passible (as distinct from *passable*) means "capable of feeling or suffering".

Incorrigible is commonly used, but its base, *corrigible* ("capable of being corrected") is seldom used.

Invaluable is not the negative form of *valuable*; it means "above valuation, of inestimable value".

The noun *force* leads to two verbs, *force* and *enforce*. The verb *force* leads to two adjectives, *forcible* and *forceful*—negatives *inforcible* and *unforceful*. The adjective from the verb *enforce* is *enforceable*—negative *unenforceable*.

For notes on *inflammable*, see page 48.

THE USE OF CAPITAL LETTERS

Spelling is entirely a matter for the written language. The use of capital letters (or upper-case in printers' parlance) is also a matter for the written language. Any study of spelling, therefore, would be incomplete without an examination of the use of capitals, about which there seems to be some confusion. Some people sprinkle capitals indiscriminately over their writing without realising how irritating the practice is to the reader. Some omit capitals when their use is justified. Some apparently think that all nouns require capitals. Some limit the use of capitals to nouns they regard as important.

Capitals should be used at the beginning of a sentence, and for the start of proper nouns—names of people and places. Personal titles should be graced with capitals, such as Her (or His) Majesty, Queen (or King) X, Lord Y, the Duke of Z, Mr., Mrs., Miss and Dr. The key words in titles of publications, stage productions and musical works should start with capitals, and so should the names of buildings, organisations, colleges and schools. These are the *basic* cases; there are innumerable optional cases in which words may start with capitals, but capitals must be used with care.

The cardinal points should not be given capitals unless used to specify a recognised geographical region. The correct forms are: "A-town is six miles north of B-town", "Land's End is in the south-west of England", and "The mildest area in winter was eastern Scotland". Also correct, however, are: "New regions created by the Boundary Commission included West Sussex and East Yorkshire" and "The largest territory in southern Africa is the Republic of South Africa".

The four seasons—spring, summer, autumn, winter—do not normally require capitals.

Some people wonder, quite reasonably, if there is any rule about the writing of "French chalk" and "French polish", as the association of the terms with France is remote. There is no rule, and a small *f* is sometimes used, but it is conventional to use a capital *F* if only because the adjective *French* attracts it. The term "French polisher" is ambiguous. A person who engages in French polishing should be described with a hyphen, "French-polisher", to distinguish him from a Frenchman who polishes, "French polisher".

While advising my readers to be sparing with capitals, I must record my abhorrence at the practice which has developed in some "progressive" quarters of abolishing capitals altogether. The results are, and look, ridiculous, especially when the sinners forget to be consistent and insert a few capitals here and there. This practice is to be unequivocally condemned. It is confusing to a child who is taught at school to use capitals and outside school is confronted by the unseemly work of self-conscious iconoclasts.

PUNCTUATION

Punctuation being a matter for only written language, like the use of capital letters, it should be considered with spelling. I shall not deal with the subject exhaustively here, however, and those readers who are interested will find a full account in my book, *The Right Way to Improve Your English*. I shall confine my remarks here to two punctuation marks which are intimately connected with spelling—the hyphen and the apostrophe.

The hyphen

The hyphen, a really logical punctuation mark, has two functions. One is to link separate words to make one compound word. The other is to act as a grouping agent.

Simple examples of compound words are *orange-box, paper-fastener* and *water-carrier*. Without the hyphen these would mean, absurdly, an orange-coloured box, a fastener made of paper, and a carrier made of water. Similarly, when the first part of the compound is a present participle, the hyphen is often essential, as in *changing-room* (instead of a room that is changing), *laughing-gas* and *writing-desk*. Without the hyphen these compounds would be ambiguous.

There is little fear of ambiguity in *copper-mining, ducking-stool, fruit-picker, manhole-cover, piano-stool* and *steel-production*, even when the hyphen is absent, but the fact that the items are *single* objects or activities, in my opinion, justifies the hyphen.

There are innumerable cases where the first word acts as an adjective describing the second, when there is no need for the hyphen, examples being *football team, herb garden, monkey house, punctuation mark* and *washing machine.* There is a commendable tendency to drop the hyphen after the combination has been well established, so that we now have, as accepted nouns, *dishwasher, earthworks, glassblower, haystack, inkwell, lampshade, wayleave; weedkiller* and a thousand others.

As a grouping agent the hyphen forms adjectives, as in *face-saving action, newly-married couple* and *public-spirited council.* Of these examples, *face-saving* and *public-spirited* are always adjectives, so that the hyphen is still necessary if we write "His action was face-saving" or "The council was public-spirited". *Newly married,* however, need not be a compound adjective but simply a pair of independent words, so that if we write "They are newly married" there is no hyphen.

The omission of the hyphen can produce absurd ambiguities like "man eating tiger", "small business heads", "obsolete food contamination regulations", "galloping inflation sufferers", "edible oil technologist" and "fine tooth comb". The logical way of writing these, as should be obvious after a little thought, is: "man-eating tiger", "small-business heads", "obsolete food-contamination regulations", "galloping-inflation sufferers", "edible-oil technologist" and "fine-tooth comb". You should have a tooth-brush, but a tooth-comb is unnecessary.

Two awkward words are *cooperate* and *coordinate,* with their derivatives *cooperation, cooperative* and *coordination.* The hyphen is no more justified here than in other *co-* words such as *coagulate* and *coincidence*; it may be used to avoid any suggestion of an *oo* sound, but it also produces anomalies like *unco-ordinated* and *unco-operative.*

The Americans have got over the difficulty by using a "diaeresis"—two dots over the second of a pair of adjacent vowels to indicate a change in vowel sound—which results in *coöperate* and *coördinate.* This is not a truly English device, however, it is awkward in typing, and there is nothing wrong in simply writing *cooperate* and *coordinate.*

The apostrophe

The apostrophe has two functions—to indicate possession, and to take the place, for the sake of abbreviation, of omitted letters.

Knowledge of its use should be elementary, but there is wide-spread and surprising ignorance.

Simple cases of possession include *Jim's dog, my uncle's book* and *St. John's Church*. In each of these the possessor is singular, and the *s* follows the apostrophe. Where ownership is shared by two or more nouns the apostrophe comes after the *s*, as in *the girls' hats, the dogs' bones* and *the two nations' agreement*.

Most proper nouns ending in *s* take apostrophe-*s*, as in *Columbus's ship, Charles's reign, Frances's doll, Keats's poetry* and *Pythagoras's theorem*. Exceptions hallowed by tradition or euphony include *Achilles' heel, goodness' sake, Jesus' sake, Moses' law* and *Xerxes' fleet*. Another exception, in which the final sibilant acts as *s*, is *conscience' sake*. Classical poetry abounds in exceptions in this and other matters of grammar, but is usually exonerated by something called poetic licence.

Collective nouns are treated as singular, so that the apostrophe comes before the *s* in expressions like *the people's homes, the children's toys, the men's work* and *the mice's hole*.

Even some journalists are confused when writing about people's homes. You write *Mr. Jones's house* or *Mrs. Jones's house*, but if you want to refer to the joint ownership you treat the Jones household as plural and write *the Joneses' house*.

Commercial establishments should receive exactly the same treatment. If a firm is controlled by one man called Smith you can write that you do your shopping at *Smith's*. If there are two or more Smiths in a family business the correct form is *Smiths'*. If you do not know how many Smiths there are it is safe to stick to *Smith's*.

I have two newspaper reports. One refers to "the Dean of St. Paul's note" and the other to "the Serjeant-at-Arm's chair". Anything possessed by or attributed to the Dean of St. Paul's should take the apostrophe-*s* in the normal way. The logical rendering of this phrase is "the Dean of St. Paul's's note", but as this looks unwieldy it would be preferable to write "the note of the Dean of St. Paul's". The other phrase should be "the Serjeant-at-Arms's chair" or "the chair of the Serjeant-at-Arms".

On the subject of place-names where a possessive is involved, the only advice I can give is to follow tradition or custom, wrong though it may be. I refer, for example, to St. Albans,

St. Andrews, St. Annes, St. Helens, St. Ives, St. Leonards and St. Mawes, none of which is granted an apostrophe. St. Michael's Mount, St. John's Wood and Land's End are favoured, but Golders Green shuns the apostrophe.

The treatment of possessive pronouns has varied in the past, but today the accepted practice is to omit the apostrophe in *hers, ours, theirs* and *yours*. These possessive pronouns thus agree with *its*, which was never given an apostrophe. Confusion between the possessive *its* and the abbreviation *it's* (*it is*) is one of the commonest mistakes in spelling. *It's* is one of the abbreviations, or contractions, in the same group as *can't, isn't, shouldn't, it'll, I'd, he's, we'll, they're. Won't* is a mysterious abbreviation of *will not*; it may be a corruption of "willn't", or it may owe its origin to the fact that it rhymes with *don't. Shan't*, meaning *shall not*, should have two apostrophes, and in many nineteenth-century books it is written *sha'n't.* George Bernard Shaw tried to assert his individuality by omitting the apostrophe from familiar contractions and wrote "didnt", "wont", "weve" and "shouldnt", but perversely he retained it in *I'm, I'll* and *he's.*

DIPHTHONGS AND DIAERESES

The definition of a diphthong has been gradually altered over the past few centuries. Even as late as the nineteenth century it was applied to a sound like *ou* in *sound* and *mouse*, which is produced by a rapid contraction of two vowel sounds *ah* and *oo*. Today, however, a diphthong (*not* "dipthong") is understood to be defined as a combination of two vowels to produce a *single* sound, which is not the same as a rapid contraction of sounds. There are now only two diphthongs in English, *ae* and *oe*, two combinations which are both pronounced *ee*. I need hardly say that these combinations occur without the *ee* sound in numerous words, but these cases are not diphthongs and do not concern us now.

Words containing the diphthong *ae* include the following— *aegis, aeon, aesthetic, anaemia, archaeology, diaeresis, (en)cyclopaedia, haematite, haemoglobin, mediaeval*—as well as the proper names *Aegean, Caesar* and *Mycenae*. In *Aegean* the *Ae* is the diphthong, the *ea* after the *g* being two separate syllables.

Words containing the diphthong *oe* are less common, and seem to be largely confined to the vocabularies of science, medicine and classical mythology. They include *coelacanth, diarrhoea, foetid, foetus, oenophile, oesophagus, oestrogen,* and the names *Oedipus* and *Oenone*. It is interesting that the word *people* contains the diphthong in reverse but with the same effect. *Manoeuvre* (not an *ee* sound) is an outsider (American *maneuver*).

The Americans have discarded the diphthong *ae* in favour of a single *e* in most instances except proper names such as *Aegean* and *Caesar*, although they have retained *oe*. In both British and American English the *a* has entirely disappeared from *aether* and the *o* from *oecumenical*.

Printers sometimes use a character called a *ligature* which combines two letters, and among the ligatures in use are the diphthongs *æ* and *œ*.

A diaeresis (plural *diaereses*) is a mark, consisting of two dots, placed over the second vowel of a pair of adjacent vowels to indicate that it is sounded separately. I have mentioned it in discussing its possible use in *coöperate* and *coördinate*, a use favoured by Americans. If the diaeresis is applied to these two words (and their derivatives) something could be said for its application to other *oo* words where the *oo* is pronounced as two syllables, such as *oolite* and *zoology*.

I maintain that the diaeresis should be used only where otherwise there may be some doubt about pronunciation. Its use in *aërate*, for example, is to be encouraged if only to act as a brake on those innumerable people who want to mispronounce the word "areate". I think that its use is justified in *daïs* and *naïve*, but one could reasonably argue that *chaos* is equally deserving. Incidentally, it is curious that the feminine form of *naïve* (masculine *naïf*) persists in English to cover both sexes. The noun, *naïveté*, is sometimes expressed in the anglicised form of *naïvety*.

Some proper names usually take the diaeresis where two adjacent vowels appear, as in *Aïda, Chloë* and *Thaïs*, but the Brontë family's insistence on it in the single final *e* seems to have been hardly justified when an acute accent (*é*) would have

had the same effect. Sir Noël Coward used the mark only in
his later years.

AMERICAN SPELLING

The following is a list of the commoner words in which
American spelling differs from British spelling.

British	American	British	American
anaemia	anemia	haematite	hematite
analyse	analyze	haemoglobin	hemoglobin
archaeology	archeology	honour	honor
armour	armor	humour	humor
axe	ax	jewellery	jewelry
behaviour	behavior	kerb	curb
calibre	caliber	labour	labor
cancellation	cancelation	levelled	leveled
candour	candor	libelled	libeled
carburettor	carburetor	licence (*noun*)	license
catalogue	catalog	litre	liter
centre	center	manoeuvre	maneuver
cheque	check	meagre	meager
colour	color	mediaeval	medieval
councillor	councilor	metre	meter
counsellor	counselor	mollusc	mollusk
defence	defense	mould	mold
disc	disk	moult	molt
dived	dove	neighbour	neighbor
encyclopaedia	encyclopedia	odour	odor
enrol	enroll	offence	offense
enthralment	enthrallment	omelette	omelet
epilogue	epilog	paralyse	paralyze
equalled	equaled	parlour	parlor
favour	favor	plough	plow
foetus	fetus	practise (*verb*)	practice *also*
fulfil	fulfill		practise
gaol	jail	pretence	pretense
glycerine	glycerin	programme	program
good-bye	good-by	prologue	prolog
grey	gray	pyjamas	pajamas

British	American	British	American
quarrelled	quarreled	theatre	theater
sceptic	skeptic	traveller	traveler
sceptre	scepter	travelling	traveling
skilful	skillful	tyre	tire
smoulder	smolder	vice	vise
sombre	somber	waggon	wagon
storey	story	woollen	woolen
succour	succor	woolly	wooly or woolly
sulphur	sulfur		

As a general rule, all nouns which in British English end in *our* (such as *candour* and *humour* in the above list) end in *or* in American English. However, the following words are the same in both: *glamorous, meter* (instrument), *coloration, honorific, humorist, humorous, laborious, license* (verb), *Saviour* (in the Christian sense), *stupor* and *tremor*. In British English *pavior* (page 44) is found more often than *paviour*. The Americans use both *practice* and *practise* for the verb.

The differences between *aluminium* (British) and *aluminum*, and between *speciality* and *specialty* (American) are differences not in spelling as much as differences in the words themselves.

It may be useful here to give a list of words of which the spelling can vary in both British and American English: *cider, cyder; cipher, cypher; fantasy, phantasy; fuse, fuze; lichgate, lychgate; mortice, mortise; pygmy, pigmy; silvan, sylvan; siphon, syphon; siren, syren; sty, stye* (on the eyelid); *wych-elm, witch-elm.*

PART IV

Notes on Selected Words

The last section of this book is a list of words intended mainly, but not wholly, as a spelling guide. There are hundreds of words, however, which, instead of condemnation to mere inclusion in a cold list, deserve comment, observation, discursive treatment. In the following pages there is a selection of such words, many of which appear also in the final spelling guide.

abjure The infrequency with which this word is used may perhaps be attributed to the rather horrific finality of its meaning, "to renounce, recant, retreat, or abrogate anything upon oath". It is sometimes misused in a sense of command or appeal, as in: "I abjure you to . . .", when the word to be used is not *abjure* but *adjure*.

accept, except To many people these sound alike, with the unfortunate result that "Present company accepted" is sometimes heard (instead of *excepted*).

accessary, accessory Few people seem to be aware that the legal term *accessary* (as in "accessary after the fact") is different from the word *accessory*, which is applied to a piece of equipment or a contribution.

adapt, adopt The noun from the first verb is *adaptation*, not "adaption". The noun from the second is *adoption*.

adjure See *abjure*.

adopted, adoptive When a child is *adopted* his new parents become *adoptive* parents.

advice, advise, adviser, advisory To *advise* is to give *advice*. A person who gives advice is an *adviser* (occasionally spelt *advisor*), and he serves in an *advisory* function.

affect, effect The confusion between these is not diminished by the fact that although the first is *always* a verb the second can be verb or noun. Something which has an *effect* on you *affects* you. When you achieve something, or bring something about, you *effect* it.

affection, affectation The first is a word for fondness, emotional attachment; the second signifies pretence, artificiality.

albumen, albumin The first is the white of an egg, the second a class of protein.

align The derivation is French (*aligner*, arrange in line), and unaccountably this form is used nearly always in preference to the acceptable *aline*. (See *gn* words.)

all right Always two words. See page 88.

ambidextrous See *dextrous*.

amend, emend These are not quite the same in meaning. To *amend* is to correct errors or make improvements. To *emend* is to remove errors from a book or manuscript.

amok You can run *amok* but not "amuck", which is a corruption. *Amok* is one of the several Malayan words in English.

analyst, annalist These two sound alike. An *analyst* is one who *analyses*. An *annalist* is one who compiles *annals*, or records of historical events.

animus, animosity The first, though literally an animated spirit, is often wrongly given the same interpretation as *animosity*, a feeling of enmity.

ante-, anti- The prefix *ante-* means *before*, as in *antedate*, *antediluvian* (before the flood), *antechamber*, and *antecede* (precede). The prefix *anti-* shows opposition, as in *anticlimax, anticyclone, antidote*. *Antipathy* is the opposite of *sympathy*. An *antimacassar* was placed over the back of an armchair to shield it from the effects of macassar oil with which hair was dressed.

apogee It is remarkable how certain scientific words have crept into everyday speech, one example being the astronomical word *apogee*—the highest point of an orbit in its relation to the earth—which is popularly used for a culmination or the highest attainment.

apophthegm I include this word in this section as it is such a tongue-twister. It means a terse or witty saying, a maxim. (See *gm* words.)

aposiopesis You may never use this word or have even heard it. It is a rhetorical term meaning a sudden breaking-off in speech for dramatic effect, a device favoured by some politicians.

apposite, opposite In a sense these two adjectives are antonyms (words of opposite meanings). *Apposite* means fit, apt, appropriate, so that if it is misread or misprinted as *opposite* a meaning contrary to the writer's may be given.

archiepiscopal Of the many words starting with *arch* this is probably the one most likely to be misspelt. The conjunction of the two vowels *i* and *e* can be confusing, and either is liable to be omitted.

artefact, artifact Archaeologists use both spellings.

artiste The use of the French word to describe, for example, a professional singer or dancer was an English affectation. At least it distinguishes a performer from an *artist*, a word which is properly applied to one who practises one of the fine arts.

asphalt This material is often miscalled "ashfalt" or even, strangely, "ashfelt". It has nothing to do with ash, and careless spellers and talkers must take careful note of the word.

assurance This has two connected meanings: (1) guarantee that something is true, certainty, self-confidence; (2) in a commercial sense, insurance, so that an insurance company may call itself the X Assurance Company.

auger, augur Liable to be confused. An *auger* as a noun is a drill, or as a verb the word describes the act of drilling with an auger. An *augur* is an omen, or as a verb it means to prognosticate from signs and omens.

aural, oral These two sound almost alike. *Aural* pertains to the ear, *oral* to the mouth or speech.

balmy, barmy These are very often confused. The spelling of the first should be remembered by its association with *balm*, a soothing ointment, so that it has come to mean "soft, soothing, fragrant", as in "a balmy evening". *Barm* is yeast formed in fermentation, and as its vapour is said to induce lightheadedness *barmy* has come to mean "crazy, volatile".

bark, barque I mean the floating kind of bark, neither the bark of a tree nor the bark of a dog. *Bark* is usually a poetic word for any ship or boat. *Barque* is a technical term for a ship of special rig.

behest "The darkness falls at thy behest." The lovely line of John Ellerton calls attention to a word which is now seldom used in the harsh world of commands, orders and requests.

biannual, biennial The first means "twice a year", the second "every two years".

billion Traditionally, a billion in the United Kingdom and many other parts of the world was a million million. In the United States and France it was only a thousand million. A few years ago it was decided, mainly by international financial interests, that henceforth a billion should be interpreted as a thousand million. Obviously, to such organisations as the oil industry and other huge businesses continental barriers do not exist, and consistency now seems highly essential. Awareness of the change, however, is not general, and I think that writers should still specify which billion they mean.

bonanza A mining term for a rich ore-deposit, first used in Nevada after the Spanish word for prosperity or fair weather. It is now applied indiscriminately to any piece of good fortune.

boycott In 1880 Captain C. C. Boycott made himself unpopular by evicting many of the tenants of his employer, Lord Erne, in County Mayo. In retaliation his neighbours and the other tenantry thenceforth avoided all contact with him and his family, or agreed to *boycott* them.

broadcast It is occasionally forgotten that the *-cast* ending in this and similar words is past tense and past participle. We hear dreadful solecisms like "broadcasted", "forecasted", but "The sky is overcast" never presents problems.

bucolic In the minds of many this fine old word is associated with good cheer, hearty drinking. As an adjective, however, all it means is pastoral, rustic, and as a noun it is a pastoral poem.

bunkum Students of history will know that this is a corruption of *Buncombe*, a county in North Carolina, the representative of which made a speech in Congress in 1820 merely to please his constituents. His speech was so worthless that the word has clung, albeit in a different form, and has even led to the modern verb *debunk*.

by-law, by-product These are often misspelt "bye-law" and "bye-product".

cadaver You may not often today come across this word for a corpse, but it still has its uses and is not yet due for abolition. The adjective *cadaverous* means not only "corpse-like" but also "deathly pale".

cannon, canon Though sounding exactly the same the two are very different. A *cannon* is a big firearm. A *canon* is (1) a Church decree; (2) a general law or principle; (3) a list of works by a particular author; (4) part of a mass; (5) a member of a cathedral chapter.

canter Pilgrims to Canterbury rode their horses at a gentle pace called the *Canterbury*, gradually shortened to *canter*.

canvas, canvass The coarse material which is used for innumerable purposes, and on which artists paint, has one *s*, the plural being *canvases*. The verb describing a search for support (in elections, for example) has a double *s*, its other formations being *canvasses, canvassed* and *canvassing*.

carat Two meanings: (1) a unit of weight for precious stones, equal to 200 milligrammes; (2) a 24th part, so that 22-carat gold is 22/24ths pure.

carcase, carcass Alternative spellings of the same word. The plural forms are *carcases* and *carcasses*.

carillon Because this is a French word with a liquid *l* many people want to insert an *i* and mispronounce it "carillion".

carnelian Although there is an alternative spelling *cornelian*, the mineralogist spells the name of this semi-precious stone with an *a*. This spelling is more logical as the Latin derivation, *carnea*, means flesh-coloured. Another word for the same mineral is *sard*, from Sardis in Lydia, one of its ancient sources.

causal Often misprinted or misread as *casual*, with which it has no connection. It is an awkward adjective formed from the noun *cause*. A person addicted to its use might say: "Inflation and high wages are causal one with the other". There is an even more awkward extended noun, *causality*.

censer, censor, censure A *censer* is a vessel for burning incense. A *censor* is an official who examines documents in search of objectional material. *Censure* as a noun means "disapproval"; as a verb it means "to disapprove, reprimand, blame".

charisma One of the most abused words of modern times. It means "a divinely conferred power or talent, a capacity to inspire followers with devotion and enthusiasm". The noun, and its adjective *charismatic*, are now applied to persons whose qualifications are dubious.

chauvinism Napoleon's faithful soldier Nicolas Chauvin little knew how his name would be perpetuated. In his unquestioning devotion to his emperor he was accused of excessive patriotism, a sentiment which came to be called *chauvinism* in a derisory manner. The meaning has shifted somewhat to imply male supremacy, and today *chauvinism* and *chauvinist* are clichés flung about by people who know nothing about their origin.

choir, quire The pronunciation of both is *quire,* although the spelling is now nearly always *choir.* The archaism is preserved in the 1662 edition of the *Book of Common Prayer,* "In Quires and Places where they sing" (rubric after the third collect, Morning Prayer). (See also *quire.*)

climax, anticlimax The true meaning of *climax*—progression to the top rather than the top itself—is seldom appreciated, but the Greek word for ladder, *klimax,* makes it obvious. The associated adjectives are *climactic* (not to be read as *climatic*) and *anticlimactic.*

comment As a noun this calls for no discussion. Its extended form *commentary,* however, has led to the establishment of *commentator,* the person who delivers the commentary. This has led to an unpleasant verb "commentate", which I have heard used by the B.B.C. and which is a far cry from the simple verb *comment.*

compass The magnetic needle indicating magnetic north is a *compass.* The instrument used for drawing circles or arcs is a *pair of compasses.*

complacent, complaisant These two words, which sound almost alike, can be confused. *Complacent* means self-satisfied, too willing to let things take their course or stay as they are. *Complaisant* means excessively courteous, obsequious.

complement, compliment It is quite common for *compliment* to be written instead of *complement*; the reverse is less common. *Complement* means the completion of something, a quantity required to make up an existing quantity to a given total. Figuratively, a well-chosen wine can be said to *complement* a good dinner. A *compliment,* as everyone knows, is an expression of courtesy, of approbation.

comprise This, a transitive verb, is *not* the same as *compose* or *consist*, and it is ill-treated every day. You can say "composed of" or "consist of" but *never* "comprised of". Correct use lies in the following example: "The United Kingdom comprises England, Scotland, Wales and Northern Ireland". You must *not* say: "The United Kingdom is comprised of . . ."

contumely, contumaceous To treat someone with *contumely* is to treat him in an insolent and reproachful manner. It is an unusual sort of noun because of its *-ely* ending, and deserves an occasional airing. The ending of the adjective is one of the standard adjectival suffixes, giving the word—despite its unpleasant association—a rich poetical sound.

council, councillor, counsel, counsellor A *councillor* serves on a *council*. A *counsellor* gives advice, or *counsel*. As a barrister representing a client he is called *counsel* (as in "counsel for defence"). In the United States the lawyer representing a client is a *counselor*. *Counsel* is also a verb, meaning "advise".

credible, creditable *Credible* means "believable" and is the opposite of *incredible*. *Creditable* means "worthy of credit".

crevasse, crevice A *crevasse* is a deep fissure in the ice of a glacier, or a fissure in the embankment of a river. A *crevice* is any fissure or narrow opening.

criteria This, though the plural of *criterion*, is sometimes misused as a singular noun, in the same way as careless people misuse *media* and *phenomena*.

currant, current The fruit is the *currant*. The flow of electricity, water or anything else that flows is the *current*. There is also the adjective *current* (meaning present, prevailing, as in "current prices"), from which is derived the adverb *currently*.

cygnet, signet These two words which sound alike refer, of course, to (first) a young swan, and (second) a seal (not the aquatic kind).

dalmatian The dog, originally native to Dalmatia, is not a "dalmation".

data It must be remembered that this is the plural form of the noun *datum*, so that you must say "these data".

decimate Originally this meant to kill one in ten, but corruption has led to its present association with general massacre.

dependant, dependent A *dependant* is a person who depends on another for support. *Dependent* is an adjective meaning "depending on something or someone". The two are often confused.

deprecate, depreciate Literally, to *deprecate* is to try to avert by prayer, but it has come to mean "to express disapproval of something, to plead earnestly against, to regret". *Depreciate* means "to fall in value", but this meaning has been stretched somewhat to include "disparagement". As expression of disapproval can be equated with disparagement there are senses in which the two verbs can be interchanged, but the essential differences must not be overlooked.

depute The noun *deputy* is well enough known, and so is the verb *depute* ("appoint as deputy"). I include this word here in recognition of its Scottish use as a synonym for *deputy*, as in "depute treasurer", with the emphasis on the first syllable.

derring-do "Deeds of derring-do". What a strange expression! The original form of this, *dorrying don*, "daring to do", is attributed to Chaucer, but apparently it was interpreted by Spenser as a noun, *derring doe* (without the hyphen), and in this form it has been assimilated into the language as an expression for desperate courage.

desiccate It is tempting to misspell this as "dessicate".

dextrous, dexterous These are variants of the same word, the first (the commoner) form being a contraction of the second. *Dexter* means "pertaining to or situated on the right-hand side", and in heraldry it signifies a position on the right of the shield (the viewer's left). *Dexterous* originally meant "right-handed", but now means "skilful with one's hands, adroit, clever". The associated noun is *dexterity*, and a person who can use both hands with equal facility is *ambidextrous*.

didactic If you are lecturing someone, perhaps unconsciously, you are being didactic. The word is no longer applied to true teaching, and many people resent didacticism in others.

dietician, dietitian Both spellings are accepted.

digit, digital The Latin *digitus* has come a long way from its original meaning of *finger*. Because people counted on their fingers *digit* was applied to numbers under ten. When the new mathematics first appeared the word was impounded and then adopted by the computer wizards. Now we have digital computers, digital clocks and digital watches.

dilapidate Usually encountered in the adjective *dilapidated* and the noun *dilapidation*, which are often misspelt "delapidated" and "delapidation".

dilettante This word, of Italian origin (the final *e* pronounced with an acute accent), refers to a lover of the arts but more particularly an amateur who toys with several interests.

diphtheria Common mispronunciation usually makes this "diptheria". Remember that the *p* is followed by *h*.

diphthong *Not* "dipthong".

discomfit, discomfort These two are very often confused. *Discomfit* is a verb, meaning "to defeat, put to rout, frustrate, thwart" (see *rout*). Its noun is *discomfiture*. *Discomfort* as a noun (its usual form) is the opposite of *comfort*; as a verb it means "to deprive of comfort, cause uneasiness".

discompose Not to be confused with *decompose*. Meaning "to disturb the composure of", it is the opposite of *compose*, so that you could say: "Don't discompose yourself".

discreet, discrete These adjectives are explained on page 55. The associated nouns are *discretion* and *discreteness*.

disinterested, uninterested There is some misunderstanding about these two, which do *not* mean the same. *Disinterested* means "neutral, without prejudice, unbiased, impartial, unselfish, not caring one way or the other". *Uninterested*, the direct opposite of *interested*, is more vehement than *disinterested* and implies the holding not of an impartial view but of a definitely negative view.

dissect Remember the double *s* here. With a single *s* the word would be *disect*, an obsolete form of *bisect*.

disassociate, dissociate As these two verbs mean the same, the second and shorter one is preferable. It is easy, however, to flounder over the spellings, and the positions of the letter *s* must be noted.

draconian Adjective originally applied to harsh punitive measures directed against the Athenians by the legislator Dracon about 620 B.C. Now used generally for any severe imposition.

egoist, egotist These are not quite the same, although in effect they can be. An *egoist* is a self-centred person, while an *egotist* (a word which appeared after *egoist*) is one who talks about himself excessively.

elicit, illicit These two similar-sounding words can trap the unwary. *Elicit* is a verb meaning "extract", as in: "You must elicit the information". *Illicit* means "unlawful, not permitted".

eligible, illegible These are easily confused. *Eligible* means "suitable, fit or deserving to be chosen, qualified to apply" (perhaps for an appointment). *Illegible* means "unreadable".

embarrass This is sometimes misspelt with a single *r* on the analogy of *harass*.

emend See *amend, emend*.

emigrant, emigrate, immigrant, immigrate An *emigrant* is a person who leaves his country to *emigrate* to another country. An *immigrant* is the opposite, a person who *arrives* in a country, or *immigrates*, with the object of settling there.

enquire, inquire See *inquire, enquire*.

ensure, insure These are not the same. *Ensure* means "to make sure" of something. *Insure* means "to pay a premium against the possibility of misfortune", and leads to the nouns *insurance* and *assurance*. See *assurance*.

entrepreneur This is given several shades of meaning by the French, who apply it even to a funeral undertaker. In English an entrepreneur is a middleman, an agent, a contractor, one who undertakes an *enterprise* (note the similarity) in the hope of making a profit.

envelop, envelope The verb is *envelop*, the noun *envelope*.

epicure The trouble about words coined from people's names is that the people themselves are often forgotten. Epicurus, an Athenian philosopher who died in 270 B.C., taught the virtues of perfection, of the highest taste in one's choice of pleasure, especially the pleasure of food. Hence someone who is extremely particular and delicate in his eating habits is an epicurean.

erupt, irrupt These can understandably be confused. To *erupt* is to break through violently, as in a volcanic eruption, or burst out. To *irrupt* is the opposite, to burst *inwards*, so that an *irruption* is an invasion from outside, perhaps by the enemy.

esoteric If this adjective is seldom used it may be because it is just what it is—esoteric. The word means "restricted to the initiated, not generally intelligible".

etiolate An attractive verb with unattractive associations. It means "to blanch", and is applied to plants which turn white if kept in the dark and to people who become unhealthily pale.

eupeptic Despite its esoteric appearance this adjective has quite an earthy meaning—pertaining to, or having, a good digestion.

euphemism, euphuism Each of these can be misused for the other. A *euphemism* is a delicate expression for something that could be offensive, or a polite way of saying something. A *euphuism* is a pedantic affectation of elegant, high-flown and would-be witty language.

euphoria One of those words which sleep for a long time and are then suddenly rediscovered and overworked. Generally it is used partly in its proper sense of a feeling of well-being, but the fact that the feeling has to be based on over-optimism is often overlooked.

except, accept See *accept, except*.

exculpate This verb, meaning "to free from blame", has been largely superseded by *exonerate*.

exiguous A pleasant adjective (meaning small, slender) which deserves to be more popular.

exotic Simply this means "foreign, attractively strange or unusual, introduced from abroad". It does not necessarily have any romantic associations, but I have known it to be confused with *erotic*.

factitious Although a different word from *fictitious* this bears some resemblance to it in appearance and in meaning ("artificial, not genuine, contrived").

farther, further In general there is little distinction between these, although a choice may lie in the context. *Further* is exemplified in "At the further end of the room" and "A further reason exists". *Further* is also a verb, as in "To further his own ends". *Farther* is more suitable in the sentences: "A is farther from London than B" and "The sound went farther and farther away".

ferment, foment These are often confused. *Ferment* is the verb to describe the chemical process known as *fermentation*. To *foment* is (1) to apply a hot poultice or dressing—a *fomentation*—and (2) to encourage, to promote, as in "foment a revolution".

filibuster Originally a noun of Dutch and Spanish origin meaning "freebooter", or one who engages in unauthorised warfare against a foreign state, this is now applied to one who tries to obstruct legislative proceedings by prolonged speaking. It is also used for the act itself ("a filibuster on the part of Mr. X"), and has given rise to a verb *to filibuster*.

forbear, forebear People who should know better often confuse these two similar words. *Forbear* (verb, accent on the second syllable) means "to abstain or refrain from doing something, to be patient". A *forebear* (noun, accent on the first syllable) is an ancestor.

forgo, forego These are confused far too often. *Forgo* means "to deny oneself, to abstain, to decline" ("I decided to forgo the pleasure of her company."). It has a past tense *forwent*, a present participle *forgoing*, and a past participle *forgone*. *Forego* means "precede" ("go before"). It has a past tense *forewent*, a present participle *foregoing*, and a past participle used as an adjective in (for example) "*foregone* conclusion".

former, latter If you *must* use these words remember that they can refer to *only* one of two items. If you are listing more than two items, the correct and logical expressions are *the first* and *the last*.

fuchsia Any doubt as to the spelling of the noun describing this flowering shrub should be dispelled by the realisation that it was called after the sixteenth-century German botanist L. Fuchs.

furore Many people seem to be rediscovering this old Italian word without, however, giving it the full value of its three syllables, *fur-or-ay*. If it is limited to two syllables it loses much of the force of its meaning of "great excitement or enthusiasm".

further, farther See *farther, further*.

gamble, gambol These have a similar sound, except for the slight emphasis of the *o* in *gambol*. The first is understood; the second is associated with spring lambs.

gipsy, gypsy Alternative spellings. The second is preferable as these wandering people are believed to have originated in *Egypt*.

gm words There are no English words starting with *gm*, but there are several containing the combination. *Paradigm* (listed later) is one of those in which the *gm* occurs at the end, in which case the *g* is silent. It is silent in *phlegm*, but sounded in *phlegmatic*. It is silent in *apophthegm* (listed earlier), but sounded in *apophthegmatic*. In *dogma*, where the combination does not fall at the end, the *g* is sounded, as it is also in *dogmatic*. The same construction is seen in *enigma* (*enigmatic*) and *magma* (*magmatic*).

gn words There are several words starting with *gn* (such as *gneiss, gnomon, gnu*) in which the *g* is silent. Where the *gn* falls within a word the *g* is usually sounded, as in *bigness, cygnet, malignant, signatory, signet,* but an exception is *physiognomy,* where the *g* is silent. Where the *gn* falls at the end of a word it is silent, as in *align, deign, feign, impugn, malign, reign* and *sign.*

griffin, gryphon, griffon A *griffin* is the same as a *gryphon,* a fabulous creature with an eagle's head and wings and a lion's body. A *griffon* is (1) a kind of vulture, and (2) a coarse-haired breed of dog.

grisly, gristly, grizzly Three adjectives liable to be confused: (1) causing horror or dread; (2) applicable to meat; (3) grizzly bear.

gubernatorial A curious adjective meaning "of a governor". As the two words are from the same Latin word for *governor, gubernator,* there is no reason why we do not say "governatorial" or "gubernor".

harass Unlike *embarrass,* this has only one *r.*

haywire "It's all haywire", we say. Apparently the wire for baling hay was often used in attempted makeshift repairs to various kinds of farm equipment, but sometimes the result was a confused tangle of wire—hence our idiom.

hers This possessive pronoun does not carry the apostrophe.

hoard, horde The first is applied to things, as in "hoard of gold". Originally a *horde* was a tribe of Turkish clansmen, and the noun has come to be applied in a derogatory sense to a multitude of people, as in "hordes of tourists".

homogeneous This is sometimes misspelt and mispronounced as "homogenous", perhaps on the basis of "homogenised milk".

hubris A word used by some writers, ignored by others, and possibly skipped by readers who have no time to think about it. It is a Greek word for insolent pride or presumption, and in Greek tragedy its indulgence inevitably led to an unfortunate fate.

hypercritical, hypocritical To be *hypercritical* is to be excessively critical of something. To be *hypocritical* is to exhibit *hypocrisy*, a pretence of virtue.

illegible, eligible See *eligible, illegible.*

illicit, elicit See *elicit, illicit.*

immanent, imminent Two distinct words. *Immanent* means "inherent, in-dwelling". If an event is *imminent*, it will happen very soon.

immigrant See *emigrant, emigrate, immigrant, immigrate.*

inflammable See page 48.

influenza I include this common word merely because of its interesting derivation from Latin through Italian and Spanish. Its first recorded appearance in Europe was apparently in 1510, when the disease was attributed to the *influence* of the stars.

ingenious, ingenuous These two words, often confused, have no etymological connection. *Ingenious*, associated with the noun *ingenuity* and with *engineer*, means "inventive, good at organising, or specially skilful". As a "switched" adjective it can be applied to something which is the *result* of ingenuity, such as "an ingenious device" or "an ingenious explanation". *Ingenuous* means "open, frank, innocent, artless", and its noun is *ingenuousness*.

innocuous A trap for weak spellers. Note the double *n* and the single *c*.

inoculate On the strength of *innocuous* it is tempting to double the *n*, but the temptation must be resisted.

inquire, enquire These are broadly alike in meaning, but *enquire* usually conveys a meaning of simply asking. Which to use is a matter of personal choice, but *inquire* is the more common, just as *inquiry* seems to be more favoured than *enquiry*, especially in the case of an investigation.

insure, ensure See *ensure, insure.*

interregnum Literally this is a period between two reigns, and the double *r* would be more obvious if the two parts of the word were separated by a hyphen. Besides periods between reigns of monarchs the word is applied to intervals between service periods of two governments or two functionaries. It has now come to be used, not always strictly correctly, for a suspension of operations, a pause.

invalid As sometimes occurs in English, the two meanings of this word have different pronunciations—"*in*valid" (noun) for the unwell person, and "in*val*id" (adjective) describing something of no weight, force or cogency, the opposite of *valid*.

invidious This is a word used by people who may not know its meaning and use it in the wrong sense. Literally it means "envious", but it has two other interpretations—(1) tending to provoke envy or ill-will, and (2) offending through real or apparent injustice. In short, it is rather a vague word and is better left alone. Anyone who says "My position was invidious" probably could not explain what he meant.

invite This is a verb. Those dreadful people who use it as a noun instead of the musical *invitation* have no defence.

isthmus This is hard to pronounce and awkward to spell.

its, it's The instructions relating to these two little words cannot be repeated too often. The possessive *its* never has an apostrophe. The abbreviation *it's* for *it is* needs the apostrophe.

jejune This is included here because of the unconscious wish of some people to connect it with the French *jeune*. It has nothing to do with youth, its meaning being (1) "meagre, scanty", and (2) "devoid of interest in life, depressed".

latter, former. See *former, latter*.

lay, lie, laid, lain The common misuse of these words makes grammarians prematurely grey. You can *lay* something down, and a hen *lays* an egg. In the past tense, you *laid* it down and the hen *laid* an egg. You *lie* on the bed (present) and you *lay* on the bed (past). You must never say "I *laid* down" but you can

say "I *laid it* down". You must never say "I was *laying* down"
but you can say "I was *lying* down" and "I was *laying it* down".
You must never say "I went for a *lay*-down" but you can say
"for a *lie*-down". If A lies under or over B, B is *overlain* or
underlain by A—*not* "overlaid" or "underlaid". *Overlay* and
underlay are nouns—thus a coverlet or a veneer is an *overlay*—
and as verbs can be used in the past tense as in "The carpet
overlay the floor".

liaison There is a tendency to omit the second *i* in the spelling.
It is regrettable that the noun has led to a colloquial back-
formation verb *liaise* (make liaison) (followed by *with*), the use
of which, though sometimes convenient, is not to be encouraged.

licence, license In British English *licence* is the noun and *license*
the verb. In American English both noun and verb are *license*.

lineal, linear These two demand to be confused. *Lineal*, an
adjective, means "to be in the direct line of descent or ancestry",
and gives the noun *lineage*. *Linear*, also an adjective, means "to
be in line or on line", giving such expression as "linear
perspective", "linear extent". It is applied also to two related
forms of ancient writing in Crete and Greece, Linear A and
Linear B.

loath, loathe, loth Three similar words often presenting doubt.
Loathe is a verb, so that you can loathe something. *Loath* is an
adjective, meaning "unwilling or reluctant". *Loth* is another
form of *loath*, and is used mainly in the strange idiom, "nothing
loth". ("When asked if he would like a half-holiday, Jim, nothing
loth, accepted the master's offer.") *Loathing* is a present
participle often used as a noun, as in: "He viewed the scene
with loathing".

magniloquent A splendid word combining "magnificent" and
"eloquent", defined as "lofty in expression". Used in an
oratorical sense it may convey a suggestion of boastfulness.

marquess, marquis These are the same, spelling being dependent
on the personal preference of the holder of the title. His wife is
a *marchioness*.

mat, matt One of our illogicalities is that while we are now favouring *net* instead of *nett profit* we cling to a *matt surface* despite the legitimacy of *mat*.

media Readers must never be guilty of the common error of treating this noun as singular. It is, of course, the plural form of the noun *medium*.

miscible There is nothing wrong with the adjective *mixable* from the verb *mix*, but as it is a back-formation from the older *miscible* (itself from a Latin root) the second is rather more acceptable and, in science, is the standard word. The negative form is *immiscible* and the noun *miscibility*.

moot point It is a mystery that so many people say "mute point" when the two words *moot* and *mute* are utterly different. A *moot point*, something to be debated, discussed and pondered over, derives its name from the Anglo-Saxon town assembly, or court of justice, which was a *moot* or *mote*, while the meeting-place was the *moot hall*. There should be no doubt about *mute*, which simply means "silent".

mortice, mortise Applied to a lock, a joint or a chisel, either spelling is acceptable but the second (with *s*) is more common.

nadir An astronomical word (opposite of *apogee*) which has passed into normal speech. It is the point of the heavens directly opposite the zenith, and the word is used popularly for the lowest possible attainment, the place or time of greatest depression.

naphtha Common mispronunciation and misspelling often turn this word into "naptha". Remember that the *p* is followed by *h*.

naught, nought Both mean "nothing". *Nought* is the numerical expression of the figure 0, while *naught* is used mostly in an archaic or poetic way, as in "set at naught", "bring to naught".

net As an alternative to *nett*, this is becoming the standard spelling in Britain as it is in America.

news This is now singular, although in many nineteenth-century writings you will find it used as a plural, as it is in French (*les nouvelles*).

noisome Unless it is realised that this adjective has nothing to do with noise doubtful spellers may want to insert an *e*. The word means "hurtful, noxious, offensive, disgusting", the essential point being that the thing *annoys* (from Middle English *noy*).

nought, naught See *naught, nought*.

onomatopoeia This is a favourite trap in spelling games, a tendency being to misspell the final syllable as "-aeia" or "-eia".

oral, aural See *aural, oral*.

orient As noun, *Orient* means, geographically and with a capital O, The East. Oriental means "eastern or pertaining to The East". As a verb, *orient* means (1) to place something in a known relation to the cardinal points, and (2) to determine one's position in such relation. The noun from the verb is *orientation*, and this has unfortunately led to a back-formation verb "orientate" which is a modern and clumsy form of the verb *orient*.

ours This possessive pronoun does not carry an apostrophe.

outwith A Scottish form of *outside*.

overlook This can be an ambiguous verb. Your house can overlook the sea, you can overlook mistakes, you can overlook instructions, and as a superintendent you can overlook (oversee) somebody's work.

overly One of the less pleasant American words which should be avoided; an unnecessary extension of *over*, as in *overly anxious*, *overly luxurious*.

paean A cheerful noun from the Greek, originally meaning "a choral song addressed to Apollo" (one of whose names was Paian), but now given wider application to include any triumphant song ("a paean of praise").

paradigm A word sometimes used irritatingly by people who delight in superior mystification. It means a pattern, an example, a model, and, in grammar, a table of different forms taken by a particular word. (See *gm* words.)

parameter One of those scientific words which have wandered into the ordinary speech of people who misuse them. In mathematics a parameter is described as "a quantity remaining constant for a particular case". In popular usage it seems to have various vague applications, one being to describe a framework on which to hang ideas, another a prescription of limits surrounding a set of conditions.

peninsula This is the noun. The adjective is *peninsular*, which some people and newspapers think is the noun.

perpendicular To most people this means "vertical", and to architects it represents a style of architecture. Geometrically, any line at right-angles to any other line, or any plane at right-angles to any other plane, is *perpendicular* to it, though it need not be vertical.

phenomena You often hear "this phenomena", but this word is the plural form of the singular noun *phenomenon*.

phlegm, phlegmatic See *gm* words.

phosphorus Some journalists seem to have a compulsion to spell this noun *phosphorous*. There *is* such a word, but it is an adjective. (See page 65.)

piteous, pitiable, pitiful The person who *pities* is full of pity and therefore *pitiful*. The object of his pity, or the condition of the object, is *piteous* or *pitiable*. "A pitiful sight" is therefore nonsense.

pn words Some *pn* words (silent *p*) are included in the list at the end of the book.

portentous This adjective (from the noun *portent* and the verb *portend*) is often misspelt and mispronounced as "portentious", perhaps in the mistaken belief that it should rhyme with *contentious* and *pretentious*.

potation, potion There is some similarity between these. A *potation* is a draught, a beverage, the act of drinking. A *potion* is also a draught, but is usually medicinal.

practicable, practical Although the meanings are not quite the same the difference is sometimes negligible, and if you use one where the other would be more suitable nobody will be shocked. *Practicable* means "capable of being effected". *Practical* has several associated meanings, but the best are perhaps "efficient" and "suited to conditions". The solution to a problem or course of action can be practicable. A person, method or tool can be practical. An idea can be either.

practice, practise In British English *practice* is the noun and *practise* the verb. In American English *practice* is both, but *practise* also is occasionally used as a verb. It is odd that the verb is applied not only to training, or learning, or trying one's skill, but also to the carrying-out of a profession. The noun has two meanings corresponding with those of the verb; thus, a doctor conducts a *practice*, and acquisition of a skill needs *practice*.

practitioner As everyone knows, this noun is applied to a person who practises a profession, or who conducts a professional practice. The ending probably developed when it was realised that the word *practiser* did not cover a wide enough field; thus, anyone constantly practising upon a musical instrument would be a *practiser*, not a *practitioner*.

pragmatic One of those words which are constantly on some people's lips—especially politicians' lips—whether or not they understand it. It has several associated applications, the commonest being to the learning of practical lessons from history and to the judging of matters according to their practical significance. A *pragmatic* approach to a problem is one which should yield the most practical result. Its associated noun is *pragmatism*.

premise, premiss The words, pronounced similarly, both refer to a proposition laid down, assumed, or proved, from which another is inferred. The plurals are *premises* and *premisses*, the first of which is applied to buildings and adjoining land.

prescribe, proscribe To *prescribe* is to lay down or impose authoritatively, or, in a medical sense, to advise on a course of treatment or medicine. To *proscribe* is to prohibit, reject or denounce.

prestidigitator This, a favourite word for spelling-bees (literally "one who is quick-fingered"), is merely a long and pretentious word for a conjuror and has nothing to recommend it.

principal, principle These two words have been responsible for countless erasures and alterations. If you want to use the *adjective* remember that the right word is that containing *a*, *principal*. Unhappily the same word is applied as a noun to the head of a college, a leading actor, a capital sum creating interest, and an authority who gives orders. *Principle* is always a noun, and refers (for example) to a fundamental philosophy, a doctrine, a rule of action or law, and a code of behaviour.

prophecy, prophesy The noun is *prophecy*, as in "He makes a prophecy", or, in the case of the plural, "He makes prophecies". The verb is *prophesy*, as in "He will prophesy" or "He prophesies". The related adjective is *prophetic*.

proven This form of the past participle of the verb *prove* is an alternative to *proved*. It is no longer commonly used, but is still applied, for example, to wills. In Scottish law a verdict of "not proven" in a criminal trial is permissible.

ps words There are many words in English starting with *ps* but with an *s* sound. All are of Greek origin, and some are included in the list of words at the end of this book.

pt words Some *pt* words (silent *p*) are included in the list of words at the end of the book.

pusillanimous An alternative adjective for faint-hearted, cowardly, lacking strength of purpose.

putative You may not hear or see this very often, but it is a good adjective meaning "reputed, supposed, commonly regarded as".

quash An abstract verb meaning "to annul, make void, suppress", often confused with the verb of physical action, *squash*.

quasi- I include this prefix as it is growing relatively popular. Meaning "seemingly, not really, almost", it finds application in such expressions as *quasi-cultural, quasi-international, quasi-scientific*.

quire, choir See *choir, quire*. Apart from its choral association, a *quire* is a quantitative paper measure (twenty-four sheets, *or* a set of four sheets folded into eight leaves).

rarefy This verb, meaning "to make rare, less dense", is not "rarify". It makes two nouns, *rarefaction* and *rarefication*.

receipt Besides its usual sense of acknowledgment of payment, this is an old-fashioned term for a culinary *recipe*. Dr. Samuel Johnson introduced the *p* into *receipt* in his *Dictionary* of 1755, but strangely kept to *conceit* and *deceit*.

recipe See *receipt*.

refuse The two senses of this word have nothing in common except the spelling. Even the pronunciations differ.

remonstrance Noun from the verb *remonstrate*, but much more. The Grand Remonstrance was the statement of grievances presented by Parliament to Charles I in 1641, and subsequently the word *remonstrance* by itself has been sometimes applied to any set of public grievances.

renege, renegue Alternative spellings of the same word. Although it is the verb associated with the noun *renegade*, the noun is heard far more often.

reset This frequently appears in reports of Scottish legal proceedings. It is both verb and noun, meaning "to receive stolen goods" and "the act of receiving".

resin, rosin Two nouns meaning almost the same, except that *rosin* is usually applied to the solid form of the tree secretion *resin*.

reverend, reverent The first means "worthy of veneration", and when used as a title for clergymen is usually abbreviated to "The Rev." It should never be used for the surname alone, as in "The Rev. Jones", but with a Christian name or some other title as in "The Rev. Silas Jones" or "The Rev. Dr. Jones". Without the title a clergyman should be addressed as "Mr. Jones". *Reverent* means "feeling or showing reverence", the opposite being *irreverent*.

rh words The list at the end of the book includes words starting with *rh*, in which the *h* plays no part in the pronunciation.

rhododendron The ending of this Greek word is *-on*, not (as many people mispronounce it) "-um".

rhyme, rime *Rime* is an archaic, almost obsolete, form of *rhyme*, and is also a word for hoar-frost.

rout, route A *rout* in the eighteenth century was an evening party, or assemblage. It is also applied to the disorderly defeat of an army, as in "put to rout". As a verb, meaning "to dig out", it is used in gardening and in woodwork, a *router* being a special groove-cutting tool. A *route* is a course taken to arrive at a destination.

scrumptious Originally applied to anything which was considered to be first-class, stylish or excellent, this adjective now seems to be confined in its use to the description of delicious food.

semantics The study of the meanings of words. The late entrance of the noun into the common vocabulary may be due to its absence from some older reputable dictionaries. It is one of those words which enjoy phases of popularity; some politicians (who have adopted it almost as their own), when confronted by something not to their liking, are apt to dismiss it with: "It's just a matter of semantics".

sentient Worth inclusion in this section as it is an expressive word seen occasionally, meaning "having a sense of feeling". A sentient person should thus be a sympathetic person.

separate It is a common mistake to write "seperate", "seperating" and "seperation", perhaps because the *a* in the middle is usually an indistinguishable sound.

sequacious It is a pity that this archaic word is seldom seen, for it is truly expressive, meaning "lacking independence or originality, showing inclination to follow in a servile way".

sergeant, serjeant *Sergeant* is the military or police rank. *Serjeant* is applied to official functionaries such as Common Serjeant, Serjeant-at-Arms.

series Both singular and plural.

sheriff Despite the frequency with which this word has been used in the past and is still used, in surroundings as far apart as ancient British cities, Sherwood Forest and the American West, some people want to give it a double *r* and a single *f*.

signet, cygnet See *cygnet, signet*.

sinister This, the opposite of *dexter*, originally meant *left* as opposed to right, so that in heraldry anything on the left of the shield (the viewer's right) is *sinister*. The ancient association of the word with evil has no obvious explanation.

sovereign, sovran Alternative spellings of the same word, but the second is practically obsolete.

species Both singular and plural.

spoil, spoliation *Spoliation* (wartime plundering, robbery or destruction) is the noun of the verb "to spoil" or "to despoil". Some people imagine that it is a corrupt form of "spoilation", but this is not so. *Spoil* is the word at fault, as the Latin verb is *spoliare*.

stile, style A *stile* is (1) part of a door-frame, and (2) the device that helps you to cross a fence. A *style* is (1) a manner, collective characteristics, and (2) an ancient writing instrument.

subtle There is no satisfactory explanation for the *b*-less pronunciation. Sometimes you hear a pronunciation *subtile*, and although it is meant to be facetious there is, oddly enough, an archaic word of this spelling which means the same as *subtle*.

sumptuary Though connected with *sumptuous* in derivation this adjective has only a remote connection with it in meaning. It pertains to the regulation of expenditure, particularly state or official expenditure, so that a "sumptuary law" should have restrained anyone's desire for a sumptuous feast, for example.

sumptuous Originally, anything sumptuous was not only costly but it showed evidence of extravagance. Now, of course, it is applied mainly to feasting, as in "a sumptuous repast". I include it here as it is often confused in spelling and pronunciation with *scrumptious*.

supererogation A difficult word to pronounce, meaning "doing more than duty requires". The adjective is even more difficult— *supererogatory*.

supersede There is no logical reason why this should not be spelt with a *c* to make it conform with *concede, intercede* and *recede*, but this is one of the delightful inconsistencies of English spelling. The related noun is *supersession*.

surrogate A noun for a deputy or substitute, especially in an ecclesiastical sense. For example, a parish vicar or rector, as a *surrogate* of his bishop, is authorised to grant marriage licences without the reading of banns.

swingeing Present participle of the verb *swinge*, which is seldom heard. It is etymologically connected with *swing*, as the verb originally meant "to beat or strike with a swinging motion". It is now used in such senses as "swingeing taxation", "swingeing cuts", meaning taxation or cuts having the effect of a heavy blow. To distinguish it from *swinging* it is pronounced with a soft *g*.

symposium I insert this interesting word as it may not be generally appreciated that it is the equivalent of the Greek word for *banquet*. The philosophers of ancient Greece observed the friendly custom of preceding a debate or a learned discussion by a convivial party, but in more mundane centuries the word has come to be applied, rather regrettably, to the discussion itself.

tawdry This common word has had such a bizarre history that it deserves inclusion in this section. The foundress of Ely Cathedral in the seventh century (according to the Venerable Bede writing in the eighth century) was Etheldreda, wife of King Egrid, whose name was corrupted to Audrey, later St. Audrey. The inhabitants of the Isle of Ely instituted an annual fair, known as St. Audrey's Fair, where cheap jewellery, gaudy trinkets and showy lace—St. Audrey's lace—were sold. Apparently the lace was so terrible that its adjective was applied to anything in bad taste and of little value, and the description *St. Audrey's* was corrupted to *tawdry*. In *The Winter's Tale* Mopsa says to Clown: "Come, you promised me a tawdry-lace and a pair of sweet gloves."

tenterhooks A tenter is a frame on which cloth is stretched to dry. A tenterhook is a hook for attaching the cloth to the frame. By obscure association—I know not why—to be *on tenterhooks* is to be in a state of suspense.

tenuity This delicate word conveys a suggestion of slimness, slenderness, and its adjective—used more often—is *tenuous*, as in "The tenuous relationship between the two sciences . . ."

terminology Noun applied to the correct use of terms, or words, giving the adjective *terminological*. Mr. (later Sir) Winston Churchill in a speech in 1906 said: "It cannot in the opinion of His Majesty's Government be classified as slavery . . . without some risk of terminological inexactitude".

terrestrial Dozens of people asked to spell this word would spell it "terrestial".

theirs This possessive pronoun does not carry an apostrophe.

their, there, they're Of these three, which sound alike, only the first two are liable to be confused in spelling. The third (a contraction of *they are*) is usually understood.

threshold A single *h*. Contrast *withhold*.

tinker's cuss I am sure that this *cuss* is different from the colloquial corruption of *curse*. It was probably the metal patch with which the tinker repaired pots and pans. "Not worth a tinker's cuss" means "almost worthless", and if his *cuss* was a curse why should *his* curse be different from the curse of any other honourable tradesman?

tortuous, torturous The first, meaning "twisted, winding, crooked", is sometimes confused with the second, which means "causing torture, cruel".

trauma One of those words which somebody discovers, others pick up and use too often, other people misuse, and eventually, from fatigue, retires into oblivion. It is a medical noun signifying a wound or external injury, and now, I understand, its meaning can include severe shock. In popular speech, however, it is used as a noun for anything unpleasant, the adjective being *traumatic*, as in "traumatic experience".

uninterested, disinterested See *disinterested, uninterested*.

verisimilitude The length of this word may account for the fact that it is seldom used. The nearest approaches to its meaning are "probability" and "likelihood", but its actual meaning is "the *appearance* of truth" or "resemblance to reality". Sir W. S. Gilbert's lines in *The Mikado* are famous: "Merely corroborative detail, intended to give verisimilitude to an otherwise bald and unconvincing narrative."

vicar, vicarious The close connection between these two words has been forgotten. *Vicarius* in Latin means "a substitute", and, very briefly, the vicar of a parish was a substituted incumbent, or one who performed his ecclesiastical duties on behalf of somebody else, perhaps a religious house or an individual. The adjective *vicarious* thus means "substituted"; for example, a parent can vicariously enjoy his son's success, or anyone watching a lunar film can be a vicarious astronaut.

victuals, victualler *Victuals* are provisions, and the *victualler* is the person who supplies them. The accepted pronunciations— "vittles" and "vitteler"—may owe something to the Old French *vitailles*, although this word is obsolete.

vilify The adjective *vile* makes the verb *vilify* (with the *e* replaced by *i*) and the noun *vilification*.

waive, wave Although these sound alike, *waive* (forgo, relinquish, not insist on) is used much less frequently than *wave*.

while I include this word simply because it is used in parts of the north of England, especially Yorkshire, to mean *until*. This use can lead not only to ambiguity but also to danger. Somebody might instruct a child: "Do not cross the road while the light is green".

who's, whose The first is an abbreviation of *who is* or *who has*, as in "Who's the best man?" and "Who's got the job?" The second is the possessive form of *who*, as in "Whose is that hat?" and "The guards, whose duty it was to protect them . . ." The similar pronunciation leads to confusion and misspelling. Incidentally, *whose* is often used instead of *of which the*, despite the fact that *who* is a *personal* pronoun,

wistaria, wisteria Gardeners and gardening books differ about the spelling, but it does not matter as the American scientist after whom the climbing plant is named spelled his name in two ways, *Wistar* and *Wister*, before he died in 1818.

withhold It is easy to forget the second *h*, but the pronunciation should aid memory. Contrast *threshold*.

wont, won't "According to his wont" means "According to his custom or habit". *Won't* is a contraction of *will not*. It should be "willn't" (like *didn't*), but has been corrupted to its accepted form perhaps because it rhymes with *don't*.

your, you're Occasionally these are wrongly interchanged. *Your* is the possessive form of *you*, and *you're* is a contraction of *you are*. *You've* as a contraction of *you have* cannot be confused with anything.

yours This possessive pronoun does not carry an apostrophe.

PART V

Spelling Guide

My choice of words for the following list (containing over two thousand main entries) has been governed by the supposed spelling difficulties many of them present, the possible confusion of some words with similar words, and, in many cases, the inherent interest of the words. If some of my readers' favourite problem words are missing I am sorry. My difficulty has been in deciding not which words to include but which to exclude, a difficulty which will be appreciated when it is realised that even a small dictionary can contain as many as twenty thousand main references.

In my list, noun plurals are given only where the plural ending is *es* or an irregularity; if no plural ending is shown it can be accepted that the plural needs only *s,* or plurality is inapplicable (as in *antimony* and *charisma,* for example), or the word (like *scissors*) is already plural. Alternative spellings, where they exist, are separated by a comma, and in *some* of the cases where the American spelling differs from the British (not all cases) there is a special indication. Where *s* can be replaced by *z* I have given only the *s* spelling for the sake of brevity (see page 85) unless the *z* form is well established, as in *recognize* and its derivatives.

All the possible derivatives of main entries are not included, but where they are shown (sometimes only as endings) they are separated from the main entry and from each other by a semicolon. The main entry is not necessarily the basic word but is the part of speech most commonly used.

Page references are given to many words mentioned in the body of the text where further information can be found.

The following abbreviations are used in the list: *a.*, adjective; *f.*, feminine; *n.*, noun; *p.*, plural; *v.*, verb; *A.*, American; *F.*, French; *L.*, Latin; *S.*, Scottish.

A

abacus; *p.* -uses
abandon; -ment
abattoir
abbott; *f.* abbess 92
abdomen; -minal 67
aberration
abet; -tting
abeyance
abhor;
 -rrence 25, 41, 52
abjure 109
abnormal; -ality
abolish; -ition
aborigine
abridge; -gment,
 -gement 33
abrogate
abscess; *p.* -sses
abscissa; *p.* -ssae
absorb; -orption;
 absorbent;
 absorbency 35, 58
abstain; -stinence;
 -stention 36
abyss; *p.* -sses;
 -ysmal
accede; accession 38
access; accessible 71
accelerate; -ation
accessary;
 p. -ies 109
accessory;
 p. -ies 109
acclimatise; -isation
accommodate;
 -ation
accoutre; -ment 29
accumulate;
 -ation 34
acetic
acetylene
achieve; -ment
acknowledge;
 -gment;
 -gement 33
acquaint; -ance
acquiesce; -escence;
 -escent 58
acquire; -quisition

acquit;
 acquittal 42, 67
acre; acreage 75
adapt;
 adaptation 35, 109
address; *p.* -esses
adept
adhere; -erent;
 -esion 40, 41, 52
adjudicate; -ation
adjure 109
adopt; adoption;
 adoptive 35, 109
advantage;
 -ageous 61
adverse; adversity
advice; advise;
 adviser, advisor;
 advisory 86, 110
aeon 91
aesthete; -etic;
 -eticism 102
aërate; aëration 103
aestival
affect; -tion;
 -ation 110
affluent; -uence
age; ageing; ageless
aggrandisement
aggressive; -ssion
agrarian
agriculture; -ural;
 -urist 68
albumen 110
albumin 110
align;
 alignment 110,
 123
allergy; allergic
alliteration; -ive
alphabet; -ical
aluminium 105
aluminum *A.* 105
ambassador;
 f. ambassadress 92
amend;
 amendment 33,
 110
amok 110
anaesthesia;
 anaesthetic;

anaesthetist
anaglyph
analysis; *p.* -ses;
 -yst; analyse; -d;
 -sing 41, 86, 110
animadversion
animosity 110
animus 110
annalist 110
annihilate; -ation
announce; -ment 36
annul; annulled;
 annulling;
 annulment 87
annunciation 36
antagonist; -ism
antechamber
antedate
antediluvian
anticlimax; -actic
antimacassar
antimony
antirrhinum
apiary; *p.* -ies
apogee 111
apophthegm 111
aposiopesis 111
apostrophe
appal; -alled;
 -lling 87
apparel; -lled 87
appendix: *p.* -ices;
 appendicitis 91
apply; -licable 47
apposite 111
appreciate; -ative;
 -ation; -able 47
approximate; -ation
appurtenance
aqualung
aquamarine
arbiter; arbitrate;
 arbitration
archiepiscopal 111
area
armadillo
armature
arrogant; -ance
arsenic
artefact, artifact 111
arterio-sclerosis

asbestos
ascetic
asphalt 111
asphyxiate; -ation
astronomy; -ical
asymmetric; -ical
atrocity; -cious 61
auger 112
augur 112
aural 112
auspicious
autobiography;
 p. -ies
avert; averse; -sion
aviary; *p.* -ies
avocado 90
avoirdupois
axiom; -atic
azalea
azurite

B

bacillus; *p.* -illi 89
bacterium; *p.* -ia;
 bacterial;
 -riology 89
ballerina
ballot; -otted;
 -otting 24
balmy 112
barmy 112
barbarian; -rous
baroque
barque 112
battalion
bazaar
beatific; beatify 36
beauty; *p.* -ties;
 -tiful;
 -teous 66, 73, 90
beleaguer; -ed
belligerence; -ent
benefit; -ited;
 -iting; -icial;
 -iciary; -icent 67
bereave; bereft 28
besiege
bet; betted; betting
bevel; -elled; -elling
biannual 112
bias; -ased, -assed;
 -asing, -assing 25
bibliography; *p.* -ies
bibliophile

bid; bade; bidden
biennial 112
bifurcate; -ed
bisect; -ed;
 -ion 39, 88
bismuth
bivouac; -acked 29
bizarre
boatswain, bo's'n,
 bo'sun, bosun
boisterous 61
bonanza 113
bourgeois; -oisie
boycott 113
bridal
bridle
broadcast 113
bronchial;
 bronchitis
bucolic 64, 113
budgerigar
budget;
 budgetary 65
bumptious
bunkum 113
bureau; *p.* -x; -crat;
 -cracy
buttress; *p.* -esses;
 -essed
by-law 113
by-product 113

C

cacophony; *p.* -ies;
 -nous
cadaver; -rous 113
cadmium
caesarean, -ian
caesium
calamine
calibrate; -ation
calligraphy
callipers
callous; -ly; -ness
callus; *p.* -uses
calomel
calumny; *p.* -mnies;
 -mniate
camellia
campanology; -ist
camphor; -ated
cancel; -elled;
 -ellation 26

candelabrum;
 p. -abra
candour, candor *A.*;
 candid 104
cannon 113
canon; -ical 113
cantankerous
canter 113
canvas; *p.* -es 114
canvass; -es; -ed 114
capercailzie, -llie
carat 114
carbonaceous 62
Carboniferous 62
carborundum
carburettor
carcase, carcass
 (-ss *p.* -es) 114
carcinogen; -genic
caress; -essed;
 -essing
cargo; *p.* -oes 90
carillon 114
carnelian,
 cornelian 114
carnivore;
 -ivorous
caryatid
cast; casting
caste
casual
catalyse; -ysis;
 -yst 86
catarrh; -rrhal
catastrophe; -ophic
cause; causal 114
ceiling
cellulose 72
cemetery; *p.* -ries
censer 114
censor; -ed; -ing 114
censure; -d;
 censuring 114
centenarian
centre; -d; -ring;
 central 29, 68
centurion
cereal
cerium
chalcedony
chancellor; -llery
chaos; chaotic
 63, 103
charisma;
 -matic 114

chauvinism;
-nist 114
chide; chided; chid;
chidden; chiding
chloroform
choir; choral 115
choreographer; -phy
chromium; chromite
chronology;
-logical
chronometer
chrysanthemum
churl; churlish
cider, cyder 105
cinnabar
cipher, cypher 105
circular: -larise;
-larisation
circulate; -ation
circumlocution
clamour; -orous 61
claustrophobia; -bic
cleave (1):
cleavage 28, 42
cleave (2) 28
clerestory; *p.* -ries
climax; -mactic 115
coagulate; -ation 40
cognizance; -ant 86
cohere; -rent; -rence
coiffeur *F.*;
f. coiffeuse;
coiffure
colour;
coloration 105
columbium
commemorate;
-ated; -ation;
-ative
commend; -ended;
-dation
comment;
-ented 115
comminute;
-ution 38
commit; committed;
commission 33
commune;
communion;
communicant
communicate; -ation
commute;
commuter;
commuting
compass; *p.* -es 115

compel; -lling;
compulsion;
-sory 50
competent; -tence;
-tency
complacent;
-cency 115
complaisant;
-aisance 115
complement;
-ary 33, 37, 115
compliment;
-ary 115
comprehend;
-hended;
-hensive;
-hensible 48
compromise; -ed 86
compute; computer;
computation 38
concede;
concession 38
conciliate; -ation;
atory
concurrent; -ly
confidant;
f. confidante 40,
45
confident; -ence;
-ential 52
conjunctivitis
connive; -ing; -ance
connoisseur
conscience;
-entious 62
consequence;
-ential 68
conservatoire
conservatory; *p.* -ies
consistent; -ency 58
conspicuous; -ness;
-ly 62
construct; -ion;
-ive 51
contemporaneous
contemporary *a.*;
n.p. -aries
contempt; -ible;
-uous 48, 62, 71
contract;
contractual 67
controversy; -versial
contumely;
-maceous 116

convert; -version;
-vertible 38
cooperate; -ation;
-ative;
-ated 100, 103
coordinate; -ation;
-ated 100, 103
co-respondent
correspond; -ded;
-ding; -dent 40
corroborate; -ation
corundum
cotoneaster
council; -cillor 116
counsel; -sellor 116
credible; -ibility 116
creditable;
-ability 116
Cretaceous
crevasse 116
crevice 116
criterion; *p.* -ria 89
cumulative 50
currant 116
current; -ency;
-ly 116
curriculum; *p.* -la
cyanogen; cyanide
cygnet 116, 123

D

dachshund
dahlia
dalmatian 116
datum;
p. data 89, 117
debate;
debatable 47
débâcle *F.*
debilitate; -ting;
-ted
decarbonise;
-sing; -sed
decide; -ciding;
-cision; -cisive
29, 38, 50, 51
declaim; -aimed;
-clamation;
-clamatory 36, 50
decline; declension;
declination 35
decompose; -osition

decontaminate;
-ated; -ation
dedicate; -ation
defame; defamed;
defamatory
default
defend; -ed; -ing;
defence; -ensive;
-ensible;
-endant 45, 48, 51
defoliate; -ation
degenerate; -ation
deign; -ed;
-ing 123
deleterious
delicate; delicacy 56
delicatessen
delineate; -ated;
-ation
delirium
delphinium
delta; deltaic 63, 69
delude; delusion
demagogue
demarcation
demeanour
demolish; -shed;
demolition 37
demonstrate; -ation;
-ative; -strable 35
demur; demurred;
demurring 25
denote; -notation
dénouement F.
denounce; -ced;
denunciation 36
depend; -ed; -ing;
dependent (a);
dependant (n.)
40, 45, 117
deprecate; -tion 117
depreciate; -tion 117
depredate; -ation
depute; deputise;
deputy; -utation
38, 117
deride; derision;
derisory 50
dermatitis;
dermatology;
dermatologist
descend; descent;
descendant
desert (n. and v.);
deserted; -ting

desiccate; -ted 117
desideratum; p. -ta
despatch, dispatch
dessert
destroy;
destruction 34
detergent
detumescent; -ence
develop; -oped;
-oping; -opment
devolve;
devolution 38
dextrous, dexterous;
dexterity 62, 117
diabetes; -etic
diagnosis; p. -oses
diagram; -ammatic
diaeresis; p. -ses
dialysis
diarrhoea
dictionary; p. -ies
didactic;
-icism 57, 118
diet; dietary 65
dietician, -itian
differential
digit; digital 68, 118
dilapidate;
-ation 118
dilatory
dilettante 118
diminish;
diminution 37
diocese; diocesan
diphtheria 118
diphthong 118
disadvantage;
-ageous
disassociate;
-tion 119
disaster;
disastrous 50, 61
discipline
discomfit; -ed;
-ing 118
discomfort 118
discompose 118
discreet;
discretion 55, 118
discrepancy; p. -ies
discrete;
-ness 55, 118
discriminate; -ation
disgruntled
disillusion; -ed

disinterested 118
disobedient; -ence
dispense; -enser;
dispensary
dispossessed
disreputable;
-ability
dissect;
dissection 39, 88,
119
disseminate; -ation
dissertation
dissociate;
-ation 119
dissonance; -ant
dissuade;
dissuasion;
dissuasive
distil; distilled;
-illing; -iller;
distillation 87
distinct; -inction;
-inctive
distinguish;
-able; -ed
distribute; -ution
divert; -ed; -ing;
-ersion; -erse;
-ersity 54
divide; -vision;
-visive;
-vidend 38, 50, 51
dogma; dogmatic;
dogmatism 41, 63,
78, 122
dominate; -inant;
-inance; -ation 40,
52, 57
draconian 119
drama; dramatic;
-amatise; -tist 63
ductile; ductility
duplicate; -ation 69
dye; dyed; dyeing
dynamo 90
dysentery
dyspepsia
dystrophy

E

earnest; -ness
earring
eavesdrop; -pped;
-pping; -pper

ecclesiastic; -al
echelon
echo; *p.* -oes;
-oed; -oing 90
eclipse; ecliptic
ecstasy; ecstatic
ecumenical 103
eczema
edelweiss
education; -ated;
-ating; -cable;
-ative; -al 47
effeminate; -nacy
effervesce; -nt;
-nce 52, 58
efficacy; -cacious 61
efficiency; -cient
effluent
egoist; -ic; -ical;
-ism 119
egotist; -ic; -ical;
-ism 119
eider; -down
electrolysis;
-lytic; -lyte 41
electrostatic
elicit; -ited;
-iting 119
eligible;
-ibility 48, 119
eliminate; -ation
elision
elixir
ellipse; elliptic;
-tical; -tically
ellipsis; *p.* -ses
ellipsoid
emanate; -ation
embarrass; -ed; -ing;
-ment 119
embryo; -onic
emend; -ation 110
emigrate; -tion;
emigrant 119
eminent; -ence;
ency 58
emphasis; *p.* -ses;
emphatic; -ally
empirical; -ally
employ; employer;
employee;
-yment 46
emulsion; emulsify
encyclopaedia

enigma;
enigmatic 122
enquire;
enquiry 33, 124
enthrall, enthral;
-lled; -lling;
-lment 87
enthusiasm;
-astic 41
entomology;
-logical; -logist
entrepreneur 120
enumerate; -ation 35
enunciate; -ation
envelop (*v.*); -ped;
-ping 120
envelope (*n.*) 120
environment; -al
epicentre
epicure; -ean 120
epigram; -ammatic
epilogue
episcopal; -ian
epitome
eponym; -ous
equal; -lled; -lling;
-lise; -lisation 87
equate; -equation
equilibrium
equip; -ipped;
-ipping; -ipment;
-ipage
equinox; -noctial
equivalent
equivocate; -tion;
equivocal
eradicate; -ted;
-ting; -tion
erase; erasure 43
erode; erosion
erratum *L.*;
p. errata 89
error; erroneous
erudite; erudition
erupt; eruption 120
esoteric 120
essence; essential 68
estuary; *p.* -ies;
estuarine 69
etiolate; -ation 120
etymology; -logical;
-logist
eucalyptus
eupeptic 120

euphemism;
-istic 120
euphoria; -ric 120
euphuism 120
euthanasia
eventual; -ally;
-tuality
exacerbate; -ted;
-ting; -tion
exaggerate; -ation
exasperate; -ting;
-tion
excise; excision 38
excite; -cited;
-citing; -citement;
-citation 33
excrescence
excruciating
exculpate;
-ation 74, 121
execute; execution;
executive;
executor
exegesis; *p.* -ses
exemplify; -fied;
-fying
exhilarate; -ed;
-ation
exhort; -ation
exiguous; -uity 121
exonerate; -ation
exotic 64, 121
expand; expansion
expedite; -ition
expend; expense;
expenditure
explode; explosion
expurgate; -ation
exquisite
extant
extempore
extend; -ed; -ing;
-tent; -ension 34
extenuate; -tion
extort; extortion
extraordinary
extravagant;
-aganza

F

fabricate; -ation
facetious; -ness
facility; -litate

facsimile
factitious 121
Fahrenheit
fallacy; -acious 56
familiar: -arise;
 familiarity
fantasy, phantasy;
 -tasise; -tastic 64
farther 121
fascinate; -ed;
 -ation
fatuous: fatuity
favour; -ed: -ing;
 -able; -ite 47
fecund: fecundity
feldspar, felspar
felicity; -itate;
 -itation
feminine; -inity
ferment; -ation 121
ferric; ferrous 65
fertilise; -sation
feudal; -istic; -ism
fictitious
fiery; fieriness
figurative; -ly
filibuster 121
finesse
flabbergast; -ed
flaccid; -ity
flamboyant; -ance
flammable
 (=inflammable)
 48
flannel; -elled;
 -elling
fledgling. -dgeling
float; flotation
fluorescent; -ence 58
fluorspar
focus; focused;
 -ussed; focusing;
 -ussing 25, 89
foetus; foetal
 67, 103
folio 90
foment; fomentation
forbear; forbore;
 forborne;
 forbearing:
 forbearance 40,
 121
force; -ced; -cing;
 -ceful; forcible 48
forebear 121

forecast; -ing
forecastle, fo'c'sle
forego; forewent;
 foregone;
 foregoing 122
forerunner
forestall
forfeit; -ure 43
forgo; forwent;
 forgone;
 forgoing 122
formidable
formula;
 p. formulae
fortissimo
fortuitous;
 -ituity 55
fossil; -ise; -ised;
 -iliferous
fragment; -ary;
 -ation
fresco; p. -oes
fuchsia 122
fulsome; -ly;
 -ness 53
funeral; -erary;
 -ereal 68
funicular
furore 122
further 121
furtive; -ively
fuse, fuze

G

gabardine,
 gaberdine
Gaelic
galena
gallic
gallimaufry; p. -ries
gallop; -ed; -ing
galvanise; -sed;
 -sing; -nic; -ism
gamble; -led;
 -ling 122
gambol; -olled;
 -olling 122
gaol, jail A.
gardenia
garrison
garrulous
gas; p. -es; gasify;
 gasified; -ifying;
 gassed; gassing;

gaseous; gassy;
 gasification 25, 36
gauge
gauze
genealogy; -ogist
generalise; -isation
gentian
geodesy; geodetic
geography; -phic;
 -phical 63
geology; -gical;
 -gist 64
geranium
germinate; -ation
gerrymander
giant; gigantic 63
gillyflower
gipsy, gypsy;
 p. -sies 122
glacier; glaciation;
 glacial
gladiolus; p. -oli 89
glamour; glamorise;
 glamorous 61, 73,
 105
gnarled
gnash; -shed; -shing
gnat
gnaw; gnawed;
 gnawing
gneiss; gneissose 123
gnome
gnomon 123
gnostic; gnosticism
gnu 123
goddess; p. -sses
gossamer
gossip; -iped; -iping
govern; -erned;
 -erning; -ernment;
 -ernor 92
gram, gramme
gramophone
graphite; -itic
griffin, gryphon 123
griffon 123
grisly 123
gristly 123
grizzly 123
grotesque; -ly;
 -esquerie 71
grotto: p. -es 90
gruesome 53
gubernatorial 123
gullible; -ibility 48

guttural
gynaecology; -gist
gypsy, gipsy; *p.* -sies
gypsum
gyroscope; -opic

H

habitable; -ability
habitation
habitual; -ituate
haematite
haemoglobin
haemorrhage
haemorrhoid
halcyon
hallucinate; -ation
handkerchief;
    p. -fs, -eves
hangar
haphazard; -ly
harangue; -ed;
    -guing
harass; -ssed;
    -ssing 33, 123
harbinger
harbour; -ed; -ing
harebrained
harmony;
    harmonise;
    harmonious;
    harmonic 63
haywire 123
hazard; hazardous
heave; heaved;
    hove; heaving 28
hebdomad;
    hebdomadal
hegemony;
    hegemonic
heifer
heinous
hemisphere;
    hemispherical
herbaceous
herbivore; -ivorous
herculean
heredity; -editary;
    heritage;
    hereditament
hero; *p.* -oes;
    f. heroine;
    heroic 63, 90, 92
heterogeneous;
    heterogeneity

hexagon; -agonal 67
hiatus; *p.* -ses 90
hibernate; -ation
hierarchy; *p.* -chies;
    hierarchical
hieroglyph; -phic
hinder; hindrance
hippodrome
hippopotamus;
    p. -ami, -uses 90
history; -oric;
    -orical 63
histrionic
hoard 123
hollyhock
holocaust
homoeopathy;
    -athic
homogenise
homogeneous;
    -geneity 123
honorarium; *p.* -ria
honour; -ourable;
    honoured;
    honorific 47, 105
horde 123
horizon;
    horizontal
hornblende
horticulture; -ural;
    -urist
hospitable; -tality
hubris 123
human; humanity
humane;
    humaneness
humour; humorous;
    humorist 61, 105
hyacinth
hydrangea
hydraulic
hydrocarbon
hydrogen
hydrolysis
hydrometer; -etric
hydrostatic
hygiene; hygienic
hygrometer;
    -metry; -metric
hyperbola; *p.* -lae
hyperbole
hypercritical 124
hyperthermia
hypochondriac

hypocrite;
    -critical 124
hypothermia
hypothesis; *p.* -eses
hysteresis
hysteria; -erical;
    -erics

I

ichthyosaurus
iconoclast; -asm
idiom; -atic
idiosyncrasy; -cratic
igneous
ignoble; ignobility;
    ignobly
ignominy; -minious
ignoramus; *p.* -es 90
illegible; -ibility 119
illegitimate; -macy
illicit 119
illiterate; -racy
immaculate
immanent;
    -nence 124
immaterial
immeasurable;
    -ably; -ability
immigrant;
    immigration 119
imminent;
    -nence 124
immiscible; -ibility
immobilise; -ation;
    immobility
immoderate; -ly
impartial; -ality
impassable; -bility
impassible; -bility
impecunious;
    -niosity
imperative
imperceptible; -ibly;
    -tibility;
    -ception
imperial; -ism; -ist
imperious; -ness
impermeable;
    -bility
impersonate; -ation
imperturbable;
    ably; -ability
impervious; -ness

impetuous; -ly;
  impetuosity
implacable; -bly;
  implacability
imponderable; -bly;
  imponderability
importune; -unate;
  importunity
impugn; -ed;
  -ing 123
impunity
inaccessible;
  inaccessibility
inaccurate; -ly
  inaccuracy
inadmissible;
  -ibly; -ibility
inadvisable; -bility
inaugurate; -ted;
  -ting; -ation
inauspicious
incalculable;
  -ability
incarcerate; -ted;
  -ting; -ation
incendiary; -iarism
incessant; -ly
incognito
incoherent; -ence
inconceivable;
  -bly; -ability
inconsolable;
  -ability
inconspicuous;
  -ness
incontrovertible;
  -tibility
inconvertible;
  -ibility
incorrigible; -bly;
  -ibility 97
incredible; -bly;
  -ibility
incredulous; -ly;
  incredulity
incubate; -tor;
  -tion
indecipherable;
  -ability
indefatigable; -bly
indescribable; -bly;
  -ability
indestructible;
  -ibility
indigenous

indiscreet; -cretion
indispensable; -ly;
  -ability
indisputable; -ly;
  -ability
indistinguishable
indubitable; -ly
ineffaceable;
  -ability
ineffective; -ness
ineffectual; -ness
inefficient; -iency
inessential
inevitable; -ability
inexcusable; -ly;
  -ability
inexplicable; -ly
infinite; -ly
  infinity;
  infinitesimal
inflammable;
  inflammability 48
influence; -ential 68
influenza 124
ingenious;
  -enuity 55, 124
ingenuous;
  -ness 55, 124
inimitable; -ly;
  -ability
initial; -lled;
  -lling 87
initiate; -ation;
  -ative
injury; -rious
innocuous 124
innovate; -ation
innuendo; p. -s, -es
innumerable; -ly;
  -ability
inoculate; -ted;
  -ting; -ation 124
inquire; -ed; -ring;
  inquiry 33, 124
inseparable
insouciant; -ance
install; -ation 87
instalment 88
intercede;
  -cession 38
intercept; -ption 39
intermezzo; p. -zzi
interracial
interregnum 125
interrogate; -d;
  -ting; -tion;

-tor; -gatory
intersect; -ction
inundate; -d; -ting;
  -ation
invalid;
  -validity 125
invert; inversion 38
invest; -vestment;
  investiture 43
invidious 125
invite; invitation 125
irascible; -ibility
iridescence; -escent
iridium
irreconcilable; -ly;
  irreconcilability
irrelevant; -ance;
  -ancy
irrespective; -ly
irrevocable; -ly;
  irrevocability 36
irrupt; -ed; -ing;
  irruption 120
isosceles
isotope; isotopic
isthmus; p. -es 125

J

jacaranda
japonica
jasmine, jessamine
jealous; -ly;
  jealousy
jejune; -ness 125
jeopardy; -dise
jettison; -ed; -ing
jewellery,
  jewelry A.
jocose; jocosity 71
jodhpurs
journal; -ism; -ist
jubilate; -lance;
  -ation
judge; -d; -ging;
  judgment,
  judgement 33
judicature
judicial; -ally; -iary
judicious; -ly; -ness
juggernaut
Jugoslavia, Yugo-
jurisdiction
jurisprudence

just; justly; justice;
-iciary
justify; -fiable;
-fiably; -fication
juvenile
juxtapose; -sition

K

kaleidoscope
kangaroo
kerb; -stone
kerf
kidnap; -pped;
-pping; -pper
kieselguhr
kilogram, -amme
kilometre, -eter A.
kleptomania; -ac 72
knave; -vish;
-very 76
knead; -ed; -ing
knee
knell
knickers
knife; p. -ives
knit; -tted; -tting
knock; -ed; -ing; -er
knoll
knot; -tted; -tting
know; knew;
knowing; -ledge;
-dgeable
knuckle
kyanite

L

laboratory; p. -ories
labour; -ed; -ing;
-er; laborious
laburnum
labyrinth; -ine
lachrymose
lackadaisical
lacquer
laconic; -ically
lake; lacustrine 69
lament; -ed; -ing;
lamentation
laminate; -ation
language
languid; -ness
languish; -ed; -ing
languor; -ous

lapidary; p. -ies
lapis lazuli
laryngitis
lath
lathe
latitude; -udinal
laudable; -ability
laudanum
launch; -ed; -ing
lay; laid; laying 125
lease; -d; -sing;
lessee; lessor 46
legacy; p. -cies;
legatee 46, 79
legation
legend; -ary
legislate; -ation;
-ator;
-ature 43, 74
legitimate; -ly;
legitimacy
lens; p. lenses;
lenticle;
lenticular 91
lethargy; -argic
leukaemia
level; -elled;
-elling
lexicon;
lexicographer 91
liaison 126
libation
liberate; -d; -ting;
-ation
licence (n.);
-entiate;
-entious 62, 126
license (v); -d; -sing;
licensee 126
lichgate,
lychgate 105
lie; lay; lying;
lain 125
lie; lied; lying; liar
limit; -ed; -ing
lineal 66, 68, 126
linear 66, 68, 126
linguist; -ic 64
liquefy; -fied;
-fying;
-faction 37, 74
liqueur
liquid; -ise; -ised;
-ising; -isation;
liquidity 37, 74

liquidate; -d; -ting;
-tor; -ation 74
liquor
literate; literacy
lithograph; -aphic;
-aphy 63
litigate; -ation;
litigious
liturgy; -gical 64
loath, loth 126
loathe; -d; -hing;
loathsome 126
lobelia
lodge; -d; -ging;
-r; -gment,
-gement 33
longeval; -evity
longitude; -udinal
loquacious; -ness;
-acity
lubricate; -d; -ting;
-ation; -cant 40
lucrative
lugubrious; -ness
luminous; -nosity
luscious; -ness
lustre; -trous
luxuriant; -iance;
-iate; -d; -ting
luxury; luxurious
lyric; lyricism;
lyrical

M

machine; -inate;
-ation;
machinery 76
maelstrom
magistrate; -racy;
magisterial
magma;
magmatic 122
magnanimous;
-nanimity
magnate
magnesium;
magnesia;
magnesian;
magnesite
magnet; -ic; -ism;
-ise 63
magnificent; -cence
magniloquent;
-ence 126

mahogany
maintain: -ed; -ing;
  maintenance 36,
  40
malachite
maladroit; -ness
malevolent; -ence
malform; -ed;
  -malformation
malign; -gnant 123
malinger; -ed; -ing;
  malingerer
malnutrition
manage; -d; -ging;
  -ger; -gement;
  -able 47
mandate; -atory
manganese; -ganic;
  -ganous
manoeuvre,
  maneuver *A.*;
  -d; -ring 29
manufacture; -d;
  -ring; -r
margarine
marquis, marquess;
  p. -es 92, 126
marry; -rried;
  -rrying; -rriage;
  -ageable 71
marshal; -lled;
  -lling
martial
Massachusetts
marvel; -lled; -lling;
  -llous
masculine; -inity
masochism; -istic
masquerade; -d;
  -ing
mathematics; -ical;
  -ician 64
mat (*a.*), matt 127
matriarch; -al
mattress; *p.* -es
matrix; *p.* -rices 91
mausoleum
maximum; *p.* -ma;
  -imal; -mise 89
mayonnaise
measure; -d; -ring;
  -urable
medium (*n.*):
  p. media 89, 127

megalomania; -iac
melancholy; -lic;
  -olia
mellifluous; -ness
melodrama; -tic
memento; *p.* -oes,
  -os
memorable; -ably;
  memorabilia
memorandum;
  p. -anda 89
memory; *p.* -ries;
  -rise; -risation
mendacious; -acity
meretricious; -ness
meritorious; -ness
mesembryanthe-
  mum
message; messenger
metal; -allic;
  -alliferous 62, 65
metamorphosis;
  p. -ses;
  -morphic;
  -morphism
metaphor; -ical;
  -ically
meteor; meteorite
meteorology;
  -logist;
  meteorological
meter 105
metre, meter *A.*;
  metric;
  metrical 63
metropolis; -itan
mica; micaceous
microcosm; -ic
microscope; -opic
migraine
migrate; -d; -ting;
  -migrant;
  migratory 40
millenium; *p.* -nnia
mimic; -cked; -cking
mineralogy;
  -logical; -alogist
miniature; -urise
minimum; *p.* -ma;
  -imal; -mise 89
minuscule
misadventure
misalliance
misanthrope; -pist;
  misanthropy

miscellaneous;
  miscellany
miscible; -ibility 127
misdemeanour
misogyny; -nist
mispronounce:
  mispronuncia-
  tion
misshapen
Mississippi
misspell;
  misspelled;
  -sspelt; -sspelling
mitre; -tred;
  -tring 29
mnemonic
moccasin
model; -lled; -lling
molasses
molecule;
  molecular 66
molybdenum;
  -enite
moment; -ary; -arily
momentous
monarchy; -chical
monastery; *p.* -eries
mongoose;
  p. -gooses 91
monopoly; *p.* -lies;
  -opolise
monosyllable; -abic
monster;
  monstrous 61
moot 127
morass; *p.* -asses
moratorium;
  p. -riums, -ria
morphology: -ogical
mortgage; -aged;
  -aging;
  mortgagee;
  mortgagor 46, 79
mortice,
  mortise 105, 127
mosaic 64, 77
mulligatawny
multifarious
mulatto; *p.* -oes
multitude; -udinous
munificent: -cence
mutate; mutation;
  mutant 40
mute
myrmidom

myrrh

mystery; *p.* -ries;
  mystify; -fied;
  -fying; -fication

mystic; -ical;
  -cism 57

myth; -ology;
  -ological

N

*(For n sound, see
also words starting
with gn, kn and pn.)*

naiad

nadir 127

naive; naiveté,
  naivety 103

naphtha; -lene 127

narcissus; *p.* -ssi;
  -ssistic;
  -ssism 89, 90

narghile

narrate; -tor;
  -tive; -ation

nasturtium

nation; -al; -alism;
  nationalisation

naturalise; -isation

naught, nought 127

naughty; -tily;
  -tiness 80

nausea; -ate;
  -seous

navigate; -d; -ting;
  -ation; -ator;
  navigable

Nazareth

Neanderthal

Nebuchadnezzar

nebula; *p.* -ae; -lar;
  -lous

necessary; -ssity;
  -ssitate; -ssitous;
  -ssarily 65

necromancy;
  -mantic

nefarious; -ness

negate; -ative;
  -ation; negativity

neglect; -ful;
  -ligence;
  -ligible 48

negotiate; -d; -ting;
  -ation; -ator;
  negotiable

neighbour; -ly;
  -hood; -ing

nemesia

nemesis; *p.* -ses

Neolithic

neologism; -logistic

nephew; nepotism

nereid

net, nett 127

neuralgia; -gic

neurasthenia; -nic

neuritis; -ic

neurosis; *p.* -ses;
  -rotic; -rology;
  -rologist

neutral; -ise; -ity

neutron 91

nevertheless

niggardly

nihilist; -ism; -istic

niobium

nitrogen; nitrate;
  nitrite; nitrous;
  nitric 65

nitroglycerin, -ine

noble; nobility

nocturnal

noisome; -ness 128

nomenclature 77

nominate; -d; -ting;
  -ation; -ative;
  nominee

nonagenarian

nonentity; *p.* -tities

nostalgia; -gic

notice; -d; -cing;
  noticeable

notify; -fied; -fying;
  -fiable; -fication

notorious; -riety

notwithstanding

nourish; -ment

novice; novitiate

noxious; -ness

nuance

nucleus; *p.* -lei;
  -lear 66, 89

nugatory

number; numerable;
  numerate;
  numerous;
  -erical; -rator 61

numismatist; -atic

nurture; -d; -ring

nutrient; nutrition;
  nutriment

O

oasis; *p.* -oases

obdurate; -racy

obey; obedient;
  obedience 41, 52

obeisance

obelisk

obfuscate; -ation

obituary; *p.* -ries

oblation

oblige; -d; -ging;
  -igation; -igatory

oblique; obliquity

obliterate; -ation

obnoxious; -ness

obsequious; -ness

observatory; *p.* -ries

observe; -d; -ving;
  -vance; -vation

obsess; -ed; -ssion

obsidian

obsolescent;
  -escence 58

obsolete; -ness

obstetrics;
  -tetrical; -rician

obstreperous 61

obstruct; -ion;
  -ive 34

obtrude; obtrusion

occasion; -al; -ally

occident; -al

occlude; -lusion

occupy; -pied; -pier;
  -pying; -pant;
  -pation; -pancy 40

occur; occurred;
  occurring;
  occurrence 25

ocean; oceanic;
  oceanography

octagon; -al

octogenarian 70

octopus; *p.* -es 90

odour, odor *A.*;
  odorous 61

oedema; -tose;
  -tous

oesophagus;
  p. -gi, -guses 103

official; officiate;
    officialdom
officious; -ness
olfactory
omit; -tted; -tting;
    omission 38, 48
omnipotent; -ence
omniscient; -ence
omnivorous
onomatopoeia;
    -poeic 128
onyx
oolite;
    oolitic 63, 103
opalescent;
    -escence 58
opera; operatic
operate; -rable;
    operational
ophthalmia; -mic
opossum
opposite; -sition
oppress; -ed; -ing;
    -ive; -or
opprobrium
optimist; -ism
opulent; -ence
oral; -ally 112
orator; oratory;
    oration
oratorio
orchestra; -tral
ordinance
ordnance
Ordovician
orient; -al;
    -ation 128
ornament; -al;
    ornate
ornithology; -gist;
    -ological
orogenesis
orthography
orthopaedic; -dist
oscillate; -ation
osmium
ostentatious; -tation
osteopath; -ic; -ist
ostracise; -d; -sing;
    -cism
outrage; -d; -ous
outwith S. 128
overawe; -d; -wing
overlook; -ed;
    -ing 128

override; -rrode;
    -rriding; -rridden
overrule; -d; -ling
overwhelm; -ed;
    -ing
ovulate; -tion
oxygen; oxidise;
    oxidation

P

paean 128
pachyderm; -atous
paediatric; -ian
Palaeolithic
palindrome; -omic
palladium
panacea
panchromatic
pandemonium
panegyric
panel; -elled;
    -elling
panic; -cked;
    -cking 29
panorama
pantechnicon 91
papyrus; p. -yri
parabola; -olic
parachute; -tist
paradigm;
    -gmatic 122, 129
parallel; -eled;
    -eling 27, 87, 88
parallelogram
paralysis; -yse;
    -ysed; -ysing 86
parameter 129
paramount; -cy
paranoia: -c;
    paranoid
paraphernalia
paratyphoid
parenthesis; p. -ses;
    -thetical
parish; parochial;
    parochialism
parliament; -ary;
    -mentarian
paroxysm
parsimony;
    -monious 55, 61
participate; -ation
pasteurise; -d

patisserie
pavior, paviour 45
peccadillo; p. -es
pecuniary
pedagogue;
    -gogic 63
pejorative
pendulum
penicillin
peninsula; -r 66, 129
penitent; -ence;
    penitential;
    penance
pentagon; -al
penultimate
penury; -rious
perceive; -ception;
    -ceptive;
    -ceptible 39
percipient; -ience
percolate; -ation;
    -ator
peregrinate; -ation
perfunctory
periphery; -eral 68
periphrasis; p. -ses;
    -astic
permanent; -ence;
    -ency
peripatetic
perpendicular 129
persecute; -ution
perspicacity;
    -cacious
persuade; -d; -ading;
    -suasive;
    -suasion 38
pertinacity; -acious
pessimism; -mist;
    -mistic
petrify; -fied;
    -fying; -faction 73
phantasy, fantasy
pharmacy; -acist;
    -aceutical 64
phenomenon;
    p. -ena 89, 129
philanthropy; -pist
philippic 77
Philippines
philology; -ogist
philosophy; -opher
phlegm;
    phlegmatic 122,
    129

phosphorus; -oric;
-orous; -phate;
-phatic; -orescent;
-orescence 58, 65,
129
physiognomy; p. -ies
123
piquant; piquancy
pitchblende
pity; -tiful; -tiable;
-teous 47, 129
plagiarise; -rism;
-rist 41
planetarium
platinum
platonic
plebiscite
plenipotentiary;
p. -ies
plutonic 64
plutonium
pneumatic
pneumonia
poliomyelitis
poltergeist
polygon; -al 91
polytechnic
ponderous 50
portend; portent;
portentous 34, 129
positive
possess; -ed; -ing;
-or; -ion; -ive 51
posthumous
potassium; potash
potation 130
potion 130
practicable; -ability;
-ably 49, 130
practical; -cally 130
practice (n.) 130
practise (v.); -d;
-sing; -titioner 130
pragmatic;
-tism 63, 78, 130
precede; -nt;
-nce 38, 40, 41, 52
precipice; -pitous
precipitate; -ly;
-pitation
precocious;
-ocity 55
premise, premiss;
p. -s, -es 130
prepossessing

preposterous; -ness
prerogative
prescribe; -d; -bing;
prescription 131
president; -dency 40
prestidigitator 131
presume; -mption;
-mptuous;
-mably 63
pretend; -ed; -ing;
-tence; -tension;
-tentious 34
prevent; -ed; -ing;
-ventive 35, 51
principal; -ity 131
principle 131
profess; -ion; -or
profound;
-fundity 54
prognosticate;
-ation
promise; -ssory 50
pronounce; -ment;
-nunciation 36, 47
propaganda
proper; propriety 59
prophecy; p. -cies
131
prophesy; -sied;
-sying; -phetic 131
propitiate; -ation
proprietor; -tary
prorogue; -rogation
proscribe;
-cription 131
prosecute; -tion; -tor
prospectus; p. -es 90
protagonist
protuberance; -rant
prove; -d; -ving; -n;
provable;
proof 27, 47, 131
provide; provision;
-ional; -ionally 38
province;
provincial 68
proximity
psalm; psalter
pseudonym; -ous;
-ity
psoriasis
psychedelic
psychiatry; -rist; -ric
psychic; -al

psycho-analysis;
-analyst
psychology; -ogist;
-ogical
psychopath; -ic
psychosomatic;
-tism
ptarmigan
pterodactyl
Ptolemy; p. -mies;
-maic
ptomaine
pusillanimous;
-imity 62, 131
putrid; putrefy;
putrefaction 37

Q

quadrangle
quadrilateral
quadrille
quadruped
quaff; -ed; -ing
qualify; -fied;
-fying; -fication
quality; p. -ties;
qualitative
quandary; p. -ries
quantity; p. -ties;
quantitative
quarantine
quarrel; -lled; -lling;
-some 53
quarry; p. -rries;
-rried; -rrying
quarter; -ed; -ing
quartz; quartzite
quasar
quaternary
quaver; -ed; -ing
querulous; -ness
question; -ed; -ing;
-able; -ionnaire
queue; -d; -ing
quibble; -d; -bling
quick; -en; -ly; -er
quiescent; -ence
quiet; -en; -ly;
-ening
quilt; -ed; -ing
quintessence; -ential
quire 132
quit; -tted; -tting 24

quiver; -ed; -ing
quote; -d; -ting;
 -tation

R

(For r *sound, see
also words starting
with* wr.)
racket; racketeer
racket, racquet
raconteur
radial 68
radiate; -ation
radioactive;
 -tivity
radius; *p.* radii 89
ramify; -fication
ramshackle
rancour; rancorous
rapacious; -ness;
 -ly; -acity
rare; rarely;
 -ness; rarity;
 rarefaction;
 rarefication 39,
 132
ratio 90
rational; -ise;
 -ism; -ist;
 -isation
ravenous;
 -ness; -ly
react; -ion;
 -ionary
reafforest; -ation
real; -ise; -ist; -ity;
 -ism; -istic;
 -isation
reave; reaved;
 reft 28
recalcitrant;
 -rance
recapitulate;
 -ation
receive; -d; -ving;
 -r; receipt;
 reception 39, 40
reciprocate; -d;
 -ting; -ation;
 -ocal; -ocity
recognize; -ise;
 -izable, -isable;
 -ably; recognition;
 recognizance 34,
 86

reconnoitre;
 reconnaissance
recreate; -ation
recrudescent;
 -ence 58
rectangle; -gular
rectify; -fied; -ing;
 -fication; -fier
recumbent; -ence;
 -ency
recuperate; -ation
recur; -urred;
 -urring;
 -urrence 25
redeem; redemption
redolent; -ence
referendum; *p.* -da
reflect; -ed; -ing;
 reflection
refract; -ed; -ing;
 refraction
refrigerate; -ation;
 -tor
refuel; -elled; -elling
regatta
register; -stration
regret; -etted;
 -etting; -ettable;
 -ettably; -etful;
 -etfully
regular; -arity 66
regulate; -ation
rehabilitate; -ation
reimburse; -d;
 -sing; -ment
reinforce; -d; -cing;
 -ment
reinstate; -ment
rejuvenate; -d;
 -ting; -ation
relieve; -d; -ving;
 relief
rely; -lied; -ing;
 -liable; -liant
remedy (*n.*); *p.* -dies
remedy (*v.*); -died;
 -ing; remedial 68
reminiscent; -ence
remit; -itted; -itting;
 -ittance;
 remission 39, 40
remonstrate;
 remonstrance 36,
 40, 132
remunerate; -ation

rendezvous
renege, renegue; -d;
 -eging,
 -eguing 132
renounce; -d; -cing;
 renunciation
repeat; -ed; -ing;
 repetition; -itive
reprehend; -ed;
 -ing; -hensible 48
repress;
 repression 34
reprimand
reproduce; -uction;
 -uctory
reprove; reproof
repudiate; -d; -ting;
 -iation
requisition
reset *S.* 132
residue; residual;
 residuum
resin; resinated 132
respect; -ed; -ing;
 -able; -ive; -ably;
 -ively; -ful
resplendent; -dency;
 -dence
restaurateur
restore; -d; -ring;
 -ration; -rative 51
resurgent; -ence
resurrect; -ed; -ing;
 -ion
resuscitate; -ation
retaliate; -ation;
 -atory 50
retinue
retire; -d; -ring;
 -ment; retiral *S.*
retract; -ion 39
retrieve; -val
retroactive; -ly
retrograde
retrospect; -ive; -ion
reveal; -ed; -ing;
 revelation 87
reverberate; -tion
revere; -nd; -nt;
 -nce; -ntial 133
rhapsody; *p.* -dies;
 rhapsodise
rheostat
rhetoric; -al

rheumatic; -tism;
-toid
rhinoceros; *p.* -es 91
rhodium
rhododendron 91,
133
rhomb; -us; -oid;
-ic; -ohedron
rhyme; -d; -ming;
rhythm;
rhythmic 133
ricochet; -etted;
-etting
rigmarole
riparian 70
rival; -alled; -alling;
rivalry
rococo
romance;
romantic 63
rosin 132
rotund; rotundity
rout; -ed; -ing;
-er 133
route 133
rubicund; -ity
rudiment; -ary
rumbustious
ruminate; -nant;
-ative; -atively
ruthenium

S

(*For* s *sound, see
also words starting
with* ps.)
Sabbath, sabbatical
saccharin, -ine
sacrilege; -egious
sagacious; -acity
salutary; -arily
sanctify;
-fication 36, 73
sanctimony; -onious
sanguinary 69
sanguine 69
sapient; -ience
sapphire
sarcastic; sarcasm
satiate; -d; -ting;
satiation
satisfy; -fied; -ing;
-faction;
-factory 39

saturate; -ation
saturnine; -urnism
save; saviour;
salvation 45
sceptic; -ism
sceptre
scherzo; *p.* -zi
schism; -atic
schist; -ose
schizophrenia; -nic
science; -ntific;
-ntist 62, 63
scintillate; -tion
scissors 91
sclerosis
scripture; -ral
scrumptious 133
sculpture; -ural;
sculptor;
f. -tress
scurrilous; -ility
sebaceous
secateurs
secede; -d; -ding;
secession 38
secret; secrete; -d;
-ting; -tion 34
secular; -arity
sedentary
sediment; -ary
sedulous; -ulity
segregate; -tion
seismic; -mograph;
-mography
seize; -d; -zing;
seizure 86
selenium
semantic(s) 133
senescent; -ence 58
sensation; -al;
-alism 67
sententious; -ness
sentient; -ence;
-ently 133
separate; -d; -ting;
-tion;
separable 133
septic; -aemia;
sepsis
septuagenarian
sepulchre; -chral
sequacious 134
sequester; -strate;
-estration
series 91, 134

sergeant 134
serjeant 134
serration; -ated
service; -able
sexagenarian
shale; shaly 60
shellac
sheriff 134
siege
sign; -ed; -ing;
-atory; -ature 123
signal; -alled;
-alling
signet 123
silhouette; -d; -tting
silicon; silica
silvan, sylvan 105
simony
simulacrum; *p.* -ra
simulate; -d; -ting;
-ation
simultaneous; -ly
sinecure
sing; sang; sung;
-inging; -er; song
singe; -d; -ing 29
singular; -ity
sinister; -stral 134
sinus
siphon, syphon 105
siren, syren 105
skeleton; -tal
sobriquet,
soubriquet
sodium; soda
solecism
solenoid
solid; -ify;
-ification; -ity;
-arity 36, 73
soliloquy; -quise
solstice
somersault
somnambulist; -ism
sonorous; -rity
sophisticated; -tion
sophistry
sovereign,
sovran 134
space; spacious;
spatial 62, 68
spasm; -odic;
-odically
special; -ity;
-ty *A.* 105

specialise; -list
species 134
specify; -fied;
-fying; -ific;
-ification
specious; -ness
spectre; -tral 68
spectrum; p. -ra;
-roscope;
-rograph 89
speleology; -gist;
-ogical
sphagnum; -nous
spinach
spiral; -lled; -lling
spirit; -ual; -ually;
-ualism
spoil; spoliation 134
spontaneous; -ly;
-aneity
squeamish; -ness
staccato
stalactite; -titic
stalagmite; -mitic
standard; -ise;
-isation
stationary (a.)
stationery (n.)
statistics;
-istical; -istician
statute; -utory
stereophonic
stereoscope; -opy;
-opic
stigma; p. -ta
stile 134
stimulate; -d; -ting;
-ation
storey, story;
-reyed, -ried
story; p. -ries
stratagem
strategy; p. -gies;
-egic; -egist 63
stratum; p. -ta 89
streptococcus;
p. -cci
strive; strove;
striven;
striving 31
strontium
strychnine
stupendous; -ness 62
stupid; stupor;
-pefy 73

sty (pigsty); p. -sties
sty, stye (on eyelid);
p. sties, styes 105
style; -lish; -list;
-lise; -lised 134
subconscious; -ness
subcutaneous
submit; -tted;
-tting; -mission;
-missive 51
subnormal
subpoena; -ed; -ing
subsequent; -ly
subside; -d; -ding;
-dence 41
subsist; -ed; -ing;
-ence 41, 52, 58
substance; -antial 68
subtle; -ty 134
subvert; -rsion
succeed; -ed; -ing;
success
succeed; -ccession;
-ssor; -ssive
succinct; -ly
succumb; -ed; -ing
suggest; -ed; -ing;
-ion; -ive
sulphur, sulfur A.;
-ous; -ic; -phate;
-phite;
-phide 65, 77
sumptuary 65, 135
sumptuous;
-ness 135
superannuate; -tion
supererogation;
-gatory
superficial; -ity
supersonic; -ally
supernatural; -ally
supernumerary;
p. -raries
supersede; -session
38, 135
superstition;
-titious
superimpose; -sition
suppress; -ed; -ing;
-ion; -or
surfeit
surrealism; -istic
surreptitious;
-ness; -ly
surveillance

survey; -ed; -ing; -or
susceptible; -bility
suspect; -ed; -ing
suspend; -ed; -ing;
-pense; -pension
suspicious; -cion;
-ly
suzerain; -ty
swinge; -eing 29, 135
swivel; -elled;
-elling
sybarite; -itic
sycophant; -ic;
-ancy
syllable; -abic
syllogism
symbol; -ise; -ic
symmetry; -rical
symphony; p. -nies;
-onic
symposium; p. -sia
135
synchronise;
-isation
syndrome
synopsis; p. -ses;
synoptic
syntax
synthesis; p. -ses;
-esise 41, 86
syringe

T

(For t sound, see
also words starting
with pt.)
tableau; p. -x
tacit; -ly
taciturn; -ity
tactile; -tility
taffeta
tailless
tamarisk
tambourine
tangent; -ial;
-ially 68
tangible; -ibility
tantalise; -d; -sing
tantalum
tantalus
tantamount
tar; tarred; tarring
tarantella
tarantula

tartar; -ic;
   tartrate
tassel; -elled
tatterdemalion
tautology: -gical
tawdry; -riness 135
teetotal; -aller
tellurium; -ride
temperament; -al
temperature
tempestuous 62
temporary; -arily
tenacious; -ly
tendentious; -ness
tenterhooks 136
tenuous;
   tenuity 62, 136
tercentenary;
   -tennial
terminology;
   -ogical 136
terrestrial 68, 136
tessellated; -ation
testator; f. -atrix 92
thallium
theatre, theater A.;
   theatrical 64
their; theirs 102,
   136
theodolite
thermometer
thermostat
thesaurus; p. -ri
thorium
threshold 136
thrive; -d; -rove;
   -riven; -riving 31
thrombosis; p. -ses
tiara
timid; -ity
timorous; -ness
timpano, tympano;
   p. -ani; -panist
titanium
titillate; -d; -ting;
   -ation
titivate; -d; -ting;
   -ation
toboggan
tomato; p. -es 90
tonsil; -illitis
tonsure; -sorial
topography;
   -aphical
tornado; p. -es 90

torpedo; p. -es;
   -ed; -oing 29
torrent; -ial 68
tortuous;
   torturous 137
trachea; p. tracheae;
   tracheal
tradescantia
tragedy; p. -dies;
   tragic;
   tragedian 64
traitor; f. traitress
trajectory; p. -ries
trammel; -lled
tranquil; -illity;
   -illise; -illiser 54
transcend; -ed;
   -ing; -ence; -ency;
   -ent; -ental
transfer; -rred;
   -rring; -erence
transgress; -ion; -or
transistor; -ise
transit; -ion; -ive;
   -ory; -ional
translate; -d; -ting;
   -ation
translucent; -ence;
   -ency
transmit; -tted;
   -tting;
   -mission 38
transparent; -ency
trapezium;
   p. -zia, ziums
travertine
treacherous; -ery
tremble;
   tremulous 50
tremor
trespass; -ed;
   -ing; -er
triangle; -gulation
tributary; p. -aries
trigonometry;
   -etrical
tripartite
triptych
triumph; -ant; -al
trousseau; p. -x
tumult; -uous 62
tungsten
tunnel; -lled; -lling
turbulent; -ence;
   -ency

turquoise
typography; -phical
tyrant; -rannise;
   -rannical

U

ubiquitous; -quity
ulterior
ultimate; -ly; -tum
ultramarine
ultrasonic
unabridged
unacceptable
unaccustomed
unanimous; -imity
unassuming
unauthorised
unbearable; -bly
unbelievable; -bly
uncanny; -nnily
unceremonious; -ly
unconformity;
   -mable
unconscious; -ness;
   -ly
uncontrolled;
   -llable; -llably
uncooperative
uncoordinated
uncorroborated
undemonstrative
undercurrent
underrate
undersigned
undertake; -took;
   -king; -r
underwrite; -wrote;
   -written; -writing;
   -writer
undetermined
undigested
undoubted; -ly
undulate; -d; -ting;
   -ation; -atory
unequal; -lled
unequivocal; -ally
unfashionable
unfeigned; -ly
unforeseen
unfriendly; -lily
unforgettable
unfortunate; -ly
ungodly

ungrammatical; -ly
unguent
ungula; p. -e;
    ungual
unguarded
uniaxial; -ally
unicorn
unidentified; -fiable
uniform; -ity
unimaginable; -bly
unintelligible
unison
unjustified; -fiable
universe; -sal
university; p. -ties
unlawful
unlicensed
unmethodical
unmistakable
unmitigated
unnatural; -ally
unobjectionable;
    -ably
unoccupied
unpalatable
unqualified
unprecedented
unpretentious;
    -ness; -ly
unpronounceable
unrighteous; -ness
unscrupulous; -ness
unseemly; -liness
unsophisticated
untidy; untidily
untouchable
unutterable; -bly
unwholesome
unwieldy; -diness
unwilling; -ly
upholster; -ed; -ing;
    -y; -er
upbraid; -ed; -ing
uranium
urban
urbane; -anity
use; used; using;
    user; usable;
    usage; useful;
    useless 42
usurp; -ed; -ing; -er;
    -ation
usury; -urer
utility; -itarian

V

vacillate; -d; -ting;
    -ation
vaccine; -inate;
    -ation 74
vacuous; vacuity
vacuum
vade mecum L.
valediction; -tory
valetudinarian
vanadium
vanquish; -ed;
    -ing
vapour, vapor A.;
    vaporous;
    vaporise;
    vaporisation 61,
    73
varicose
variegated
vary; -ried; -rying;
    -riable; -riation;
    -rious; -riety 59
vegetable; -tate;
    -tation; -tarian 70
vehement; -mence;
    -mency
vehicle; -icular 66
vengeance 53
vengeful; -fully;
    -fulness 53
venom; -ous
vendetta
ventilate; -ation
ventriloquist; -ism;
    -loquial
veracious; -acity
veranda, verandah
verbatim
verbose; -bosity 72
verdigris
verisimilitude 137
verity; veritable
vermicelli
vermilion
vermin; -ous
vernacular
versatile; -ility
vertical; -ity
vertigo; -tiginous 62
vestibule
vestige; -igial
veterinary; -inarian

vex; -atious; -ation;
    vexed; vexing
vibrate; -d; -ating;
    -rant; -ratory 52
vicar; vicarious;
    vicarage 137
vice; vicious
vice (tool), vise A.
vicissitude
victory; p. -ries;
    -torious
victuals;
    victualler 137
vigil; -ant; -ance;
    -ante
vile; vilify;
    -lification 137
vindicate; -d; -ting;
    -ation
vindictive; -ness; -ly
viol; viola; violin;
    violoncello
virago; p. -oes
virulent; -ence
visa; -aed, a'd
viscera; -l; -te
viscous; viscosity
visible; -bly;
    visibility
visual; -ally;
    -ise; -isation
vital; -ise; -ity
vitiate; -d; -ting;
    -ation
vitreous; vitrify;
    vitrifaction;
    vitrification
vituperation
vivacious; -acity
vivisection
vocabulary; p. -ries
vocal; -cally;
    vocalist
vocation; -al; -ally
vociferate; -tion;
    -rous
volatile; -tilise;
    -tility
volcano; p. -es;
    -anic;
    volcanology,
    vulcanology;
    -ogist 90
voluble; -ubility

volume; -minous;
  -tric
volunteer;
  -untary 65
voracious; -acity
vortex; *p.* -tices;
  vortiginous
vouchsafe
vulnerable; -bility

W

wainscot; -ing
waive; -d; -ving;
  -r 138
wallaby; *p.* -bies
wallop; -ed; -ing
walrus; *p.* -es
wanton; -ness; -ly
warrant; -ed; -ing;
  -able; -y
wassail; -ailing
wave; -d; -ving 138
waver; -ed; -ing;
  waverer
wayfarer
wayward; -ness; -ly
weak; -ened; -ening;
  -ly; -ling
weasel
weave; wove;
  woven;
  weaving 28
weigh; -ed; -ing
weight; -y; -ily;
  -less
weevil; -lled; -lly
wharf; *p.* -fs, -rves;
  wharfage
wheedle; -d; -ling;
  -r
wherewithal
whereabouts
whet; -tted; -tting;
  whetstone
while; whilst 138
whinny; -nied;
  -nying
whisky; *p.* -kies
wholesome; -ness;
  -ly 53
who's 138
whose 138

wilderness; *p.* -es
will; -ed; -ing;
  -ingly; wilful 67
winsome; -ness;
  -ly 53
wiseacre
wistaria,
  wisteria 138
wit; witty; witticism;
  witted; witless
wit (*v.*); witting;
  wittingly 57
witch-elm,
  wych-elm 105
withdraw; -drew;
  -n; -ing; -al 42
withhold; -held;
  -holding 138
withstand; -stood;
  -ing
witness; *p.* -es;
  -ed; -ing
wizened
woebegone
wolfram
wonder; -ed; -ing;
  -ful;
  wondrous 50, 61,
  66
wont; -ed 138
won't 138
wool; woollen;
  woolly 71, 88
wrath; -ful
wreath
wreathe; -d; -thing
wrench; -ed; -ing
wrestle; -d; -ling; -r
wriggle; -d; -ling;
  wriggler
write; wrote;
  written; writing;
  writer
writhe; -d; -thing
wroth

X

xanthic;
  xanthate
xenophobe; -bia;
  -bic

Xerxes
xylonite
xylophone

Y

yacht; -ing
yashmak
yearn; -ed; -ing
year; -ly; -ling
yeast
yeoman; *p.* -men;
  yeomanry
yesterday
yield; -ed; -ing
yoga
yoghourt, -hurt
yoke
yolk
young; -ster 59, 78
your; yours 102, 138
you're 138
yourself;
  p. -selves
youth; -ful;
  -hood
ytterbium
yttrium
Yugoslavia,
  Jugo-

Z

zabaglione
zany
zeal; -ous; -ously
zebra
zenith
zeolite
zephyr
zeppelin
zero
zest
zinc
zinnia
zircon; zirconium
zither
zodiac; -al
zone; zonal
zoo; zoology;
  zoological;
  zoologist